Praise for

A PRINCESS STORY

from moms, grandmas, and women just like you

"Such an incredible personal adventure! This book will transform your perspective and life forever! Find out how to finally reach your happily ever after!"

—Crystal K.

"I have never read a book that has had such an impact on my life! Although it is written for women, I told my husband he needs to read it. Jaci shares some extremely powerful insights on the scriptures. If you are like me and have struggled with putting off the natural man and becoming Christlike, then you need to read this book. You will see your Savior in a whole new light!"

—Sarah M.

"Words cannot describe this powerful book! It is both inspired and inspiring. Jaci masterfully lays out powerful doctrine, yet does so in a simple way that is easily understandable and relatable by women both young and old. I kept waiting for the 'boring' part; however, chapter after chapter, I was on the edge of my seat. Cover to cover, this is a must-read! This second time through, I am reading it with my own young daughter. I found the additional study sections as an invitation to change and understand the gospel in my own personal life. I highly recommend this book to anyone seeking to better understand the great plan of happiness."

—Katy W.

"This amazing book will guide you in turning your 'dragon nature' into divine nature. And more, it will leave you with an overwhelming desire to strengthen your relationship with the Prince, who is devoted to rescuing you. I wish I had read this book as a teenager, but its message is for all ages, and I'm eager to read it again. And again."

—Julie S.

"Jaci's knowledge of the scriptures and the way we can apply them personally in our everyday lives is refreshing, and her enthusiasm about living the gospel is contagious! Every time I opened this book, I had a surge of joy and hope that becoming one with my Savior can be a reality. Besides young women, adults can benefit greatly from her easy-to-understand insights. The analogies she used helped me understand what my relationship with my Savior should be. A wonderful, empowering book!"

—Wendi B.

"This is a great self-improvement book that takes the classic princess tale and brings wonderful gospel truths to the story. I love that it has references at the end of each chapter so you can really dive in and study more of the material. It has given me a different and better understanding and insight into basic gospel principles. I loved it!"

—Katherine H.

A PRINCESS STORY

A PRINCESS STORY

The Real-Life
Fairy Tale
Found in the Gospel
of Jesus Christ

JACI WIGHTMAN

CFI
An Imprint of Cedar Fort, Inc.
Springville, UT

This is not an official publication of The Church of Jesus Christ of Latter-day Saints. The opinions and views expressed herein belong solely to the authors and do not necessarily represent the opinions or views of Cedar Fort, Inc. Permission for the use of sources, graphics, and photos is also solely the responsibility of the authors.

ISBN 13: 978-1-4621-1718-5

Published by CFI, an imprint of Cedar Fort, Inc.
2373 W. 700 S., Springville, UT 84663
Distributed by Cedar Fort, Inc., www.cedarfort.com

Library of Congress Cataloging-in-Publication Data

Wightman, Jaci, 1971- author.
A princess story : the real-life fairy tale found in the gospel of Jesus Christ / Jaci Wightman.
    pages cm
Includes bibliographical references.
ISBN 978-1-4621-1718-5 (perfect bound : alk. paper)
1. Women--Religious aspects--Church of Jesus Christ of Latter-day Saints. 2. Church of Jesus Christ of Latter-day Saints--Doctrines. 3. Mormon Church--Doctrines. I. Title.
BX8643.W66W54 2015
248.8'43088289332--dc23
                                2015027444

Cover design by Shawnda T. Craig
Cover design © 2015 Cedar Fort, Inc.
Edited and typeset by Jessica B. Ellingson

Printed in the United States of America

10 9 8 7 6 5 4 3 2 1

Printed on acid-free paper

This book is dedicated to the Rexburg 19th Ward young women and leaders from 2012–2014. I'll never forget the fun we had bringing this princess story to life. It's your love and support that truly made this whole adventure possible!

CONTENTS

Princess Movies Referenced xiii

A Short Little Intro...1

A Royal Obsession 3

A Peculiar Princess...7

A Notorious Villain 13

An Awful Monster 19

A Dragon Nature 29

An Awe-Inspiring Hero 41

A Dangerous Distraction 53

A Load of Lies 63

A Broken Heart...75

A Closer Look..87

A Great Exchange 107

A Baptism of Fire 117

A Princess Warrior...129

An Epic Battle...143

A Prince's Kingdom 159

An Endowment of Power...167

A Happily Ever After 175

Endnotes 181

Acknowledgments 191

About the Author..193

PRINCESS MOVIES REFERENCED

Tangled, directed by Nathan Greno and Byron Howard (Burbank, California: Walt Disney Animation Studios, 2010).

The Little Mermaid, directed by Ron Clements and John Musker (Burbank, California: Walt Disney Animation Studios, 1989).

Cinderella, directed by Clyde Geronimi, Hamilton Luske, and Wilfred Jackson (Burbank, California: Walt Disney Animation Studios, 1950).

Ella Enchanted, directed by Tommy O'Haver (New York: Jane Startz Productions; Dublin, Ireland: Blessington Film Productions, 2004).

Snow White and the Seven Dwarfs, directed by David Hand (Burbank, California: Walt Disney Animation Studios, 1937).

The Princess Bride, directed by Rob Reiner (ACT III Communications, 1987).

Beauty and the Beast, directed by Gary Trousdale and Kirk Wise (Burbank, California: Walt Disney Animation Studios, 1991).

Star Wars: Episode IV: A New Hope, directed by George Lucas (San Francisco, California: Lucasfilm Ltd, 1977).

Aladdin, directed by Ron Clements and John Musker (Burbank, California: Walt Disney Animation Studios, 1992).

A SHORT LITTLE INTRO

B ELIEVE IT OR not, this book came to life as I sat watching an animated princess movie with my daughters. At the time, I was a brand-new Young Women president who was trying to find a way to make the gospel more relatable to the girls in my ward. And that night, it hit me that there was a ton of gospel symbolism woven into that one simple little story. I thought it might be fun to integrate those ideas into my next Sunday lesson, and in that moment, the first scene of *A Princess Story* was born (only I didn't know it at the time).

Honestly, I never thought the idea would go beyond that one lesson, but it struck such a chord with the girls. I knew I had to keep the story going. As I continued to incorporate the ideas into my lessons, the gospel soon began to feel like much more than just going to church every Sunday. It began to feel like *an adventure*—an epic tale of a princess who was taken prisoner and the prince who came to her rescue, an intense saga filled with danger, drama, and even a little magic. To my surprise, the lessons kept building on each other for more than two years. By then I knew I had something special I wanted to share with other women, both young and old. So I pulled out my laptop and started to write.

However, you need to know right from the start that this isn't meant to be a story you read. It's meant to be a story that you *experience*. In other words, I'm hoping each and every scene will come alive in a real and interactive way. One of the best ways you can make it personal is by grabbing a journal or notebook (maybe a really cute one, if you're so inclined) and scribbling down thoughts and notes as you go along. Also, at the end of each scene, you'll find additional questions, quotes, and scriptures you can study in case you want to dive a little deeper. And you'll use your journal quite a bit in the final scenes of the story, so that's another reason to keep it close by as you read.

Basically, what I'm saying is this: you've been blessed with a really incredible imagination, so it's time to put it to work just like you would with any good fairy tale. After all, haven't you always wanted to be part of a heroic drama? Well, the time has finally come. I'll explain exactly how it works as we go along. I believe you'll soon see that this isn't a make-believe fairy tale at all but the true story of why you're here on earth and what must happen in order for you to return to the presence of your Father in Heaven.

With that said, let's go ahead and dive right in!

A ROYAL OBSESSION

ADMIT IT—AT SOME point during your childhood, didn't you dress up like a princess? Didn't you don a pink satin-like gown and plop a shiny plastic tiara on top of your head? Many little girls spend happy afternoons pretending to ride in fancy carriages, wear valuable jewels, and live in a gigantic mansion. A princess's life is the stuff that dreams are made of. Okay, maybe not. Maybe you loved to dress up like a cowgirl or a superhero instead. (That description definitely fits one of my daughters!) But that doesn't change the fact that the world today seems to be caught up in a frenzy of all things princess. To the casual observer, it may appear that princesses have taken over the entire world.

Just take a stroll through the store, and you'll find princess storybooks, princess bandages, princess makeup, princess fishing poles, princess dog chews, and princess snacks. In my local store, I even found an inflatable princess bathtub and a princess laptop that can teach you the ABCs. But I think the greatest evidence of our obsession is all those princess movies we grew up watching. I bet you've seen them more times than you can count. You may even know every single lyric to every single song, whether you like it or not. Could it be that we're captivated by these characters because deep down we love the whole idea of *being* a princess?

It wasn't all that different when I was growing up. I remember when I was a teenager back in the 1980s, and the whole world went nuts when England's Prince Charles married Lady Diana. Over 750 million people stopped their busy lives to watch it on TV. But it wasn't just the wedding that intrigued everyone—it was Diana herself. People packed the streets of London just to catch a glimpse of her. And after the wedding, things didn't calm down for Diana. Reporters commented on every outfit she wore and followed her every time she set foot out of the palace. At the time, she was one of the most photographed women in the entire world.

But the reaction to Diana was tame compared to the wedding of her son William and the beautiful Kate Middleton at Westminster Abbey. Three billion (yes, I said *billion*) people in 180 countries caught it on TV, on the radio, or online.[1] I'm sure you've seen a few pictures of Kate while standing in the checkout line at the grocery store. You'd think we'd eventually get tired of all the dramatic headlines and royal garb, but for some reason, we don't. Throw a princess story at us, and we'll stop whatever we're doing to soak it all in.

The movie *Tangled* is a perfect example. In 2010 when it was released, the film earned over $86 million in the first weekend— the biggest Thanksgiving holiday opening ever recorded up to that time.[2] That means even after Cinderella, Belle, Aurora, Jasmine, Ariel, and Snow White, the world still flocked to theaters in huge numbers to see *one more* princess movie. Then most of us hurried to buy the DVD as well. (I'll confess that one of my daughters loved *Tangled* so much, she watched it *nine times* the week we bought it. And she was in junior high at the time!) It just goes to show that when it comes to a good princess story, many of us can't get enough.

Have you ever noticed that those princess movies always seem to follow a similar storyline? Think about it: First we're introduced to a beautiful princess who sings us a spunky opening song accompanied by a number of chubby-faced animals. As she tells us of her longings, her hopes, and her dreams, we often find the same feelings hidden deep inside of us. Sadly, the reverie doesn't last for very long. Soon the scene changes and we find ourselves face-to-face with the evil villain—the wicked, conniving character who's stirring up trouble and making life miserable for the princess. We watch in horror as this awful scoundrel devises a scheme to destroy the princess's happiness forever. As a result, the princess eventually encounters some sort of danger, and often her very life is threatened.

And that, of course, is the entrance cue for the next important character. No doubt you already know who it is. Yep, you guessed it—it's the handsome prince. As we all know, this enchanting young man (who is either already a prince or will become one before the movie is over) shows up just in time to save the day. This incredible character risks his life to rescue the princess from the clutches of the dangerous villain. One look at the dashing hero and most girls can't help but daydream of the Prince Charming they hope will come charging boldly into their lives someday. Once the villain is vanquished and the danger has passed, it's time for the final scene of the story, otherwise known as the "happily ever after." As I'm sure you know, in most princess movies that involves a big, fancy wedding (or at least the promise that one will soon be coming).

Can you see how, in movie after movie, the exact same pattern is played out again and again? While each story has its own twists and turns, princess movies always seem to include a princess, a villain, some danger, a prince who comes to the rescue, and a happy ending. And like I said, for some reason we never get tired of that particular fairy tale. We *want* to see the prince rescue the princess. We *want* to see the villain go down in flames. We *want* to see the couple live happily ever after. It gives us our own little moment of bliss every time we walk out of the theater or turn off the DVD player.

With that said, I believe we're drawn to these stories not just because they're full of adventure and romance or because they're packed with funny one-liners and great music, but because the storyline is actually *real*. I'm not kidding. Now, I'm not saying that the animated characters are real. I'm saying that the *pattern* found in princess movies (meaning the princess, the prince, the villain, the heroic rescue, and the happily ever after) is real—and

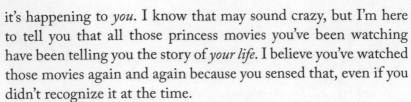

it's happening to *you*. I know that may sound crazy, but I'm here to tell you that all those princess movies you've been watching have been telling you the story of *your life*. I believe you've watched those movies again and again because you sensed that, even if you didn't recognize it at the time.

If you have absolutely no idea what I'm talking about, don't worry. I'm going to show you step by step how each part of the princess pattern fits your life and your individual circumstances. But before we begin, let me warn you: If you think you already know how the story goes, it's time to think again. Even if you've seen those princess movies a hundred times, the details of your own story may surprise you. As the tale unfolds, you're going to find some unexpected twists and turns and some danger you probably didn't even know existed. But the good news is that your story also has a better ending than any fairy tale you've ever heard. Get ready for a beautiful story of princes and princesses, villains and dragons, and an incredibly daring rescue. By the time we're through, I'm hoping you'll never see a princess movie the same way again.

A PECULIAR PRINCESS

ONCE UPON A time, there lived a beautiful princess. Isn't that how every single princess story starts? What's different this time is that *you're* the one who gets to step into the starring role. If you can't see yourself as a member of a royal family, consider what President Dieter F. Uchtdorf said in a talk given specifically to the young women of the Church: "You are truly royal spirit daughters of Almighty God. *You are princesses, destined to become queens.* Your own wondrous story has already begun. Your 'once upon a time' is now."[1]

Amazing, isn't it? President Uchtdorf just proved my point: you really are a princess. You're the daughter of a magnificent heavenly King. In fact, in the same broadcast where President Uchtdorf said those words, Young Women general president Elaine S. Dalton shared this similar thought: "Each of you has inherited a royal birthright. Each of you has a divine heritage. . . . *Each of you was born to be a queen.*"[2]

If you grew up in the Church, I'm guessing you've heard this idea many times over the years. But even so, I want you to take a minute to let this glorious truth sink deep into your heart. It's true, you know. You really are a princess. It's not just a make-believe role in a make-believe story. A long time ago before you even came to this world, you lived in the celestial mansion of a heavenly King

and Queen. And like all children of royal birth, you were trea-sured, adored, and lavished with divine love and affection.

Yet as wonderful as it is to contemplate your amazing pre-mortal life, it may be frustrating too, because you can't remember anything about it. You probably know why that is. As President Uchtdorf tells us, "A veil separates this mortality from our heav-enly home."[3] That means for the time being, your memory of your former home is hidden from you. Our Father in Heaven does this so life on earth will be a true test, and so you can learn to exer-cise faith in Him and His wonderful plan of happiness. But that doesn't mean you don't know anything at all about your premortal past. No, I'm guessing your parents, leaders, and teachers have worked hard to help you understand who you really are.

For example, how old were you when you were taught to sing "I Am a Child of God"? Maybe three or four? Even at that tiny age, your parents and teachers were using music to teach you about your divine heritage. As you grew, you probably also heard family home evening lessons, sharing time presentations, and general conference talks that explained the truth about your heavenly parents. And when you moved into Young Women, your lead-ers continued to remind you again and again that you really are a princess—a future queen and royal daughter of God.

To illustrate, think about the first phrase of the Young Women theme, repeated every Sunday by girls all over the world. You probably know the words by heart: "We are daughters of our Heavenly Father, who loves us, and we love Him."[4] Notice that the theme starts out first and foremost by reminding you who you really are. The first page of *For the Strength of Youth* does the same thing when it says, "You are beloved . . . daughters of God and He is mindful of you."[5] And the Personal Progress booklet also opens with a similar statement: "You are a beloved daughter of Heavenly Father, prepared to come to the earth at this particular time for a sacred and glorious purpose."[6] While the idea of being a daughter of God may not be new to you, what you need to remember is that your Father in Heaven isn't just a God—He's also an exalted, heavenly King (see Psalms 45:6 and 95:3). So as His child, that really does make you a princess. Like Sister Dalton said, you really were born to be a queen.

You might be surprised to learn that my Church leaders told me the same thing when I was growing up. For instance, in 1986 when I was fifteen years old, President Ezra Taft Benson said this in a talk given to young women:

> You have been born at this time for a sacred and glorious purpose. It is not by chance that you have been reserved to come to earth in this last dispensation of the fulness of times. Your birth at this particular time was foreordained in the eternities.
>
> You are to be the royal daughters of the Lord in the last days. You are 'youth of the noble birthright.'[7]

Now, I have to admit that even though I loved the prophet and knew his words were true, I still didn't feel much like a princess. I didn't feel amazing or royal or special or spectacular—I just felt ordinary (or sometimes, even less than ordinary). In fact, with all the teenage drama I dealt with on a daily basis, I often felt more like Cinderella in her rags than Kate in her gorgeous wedding dress. Though I understood in my head that I was the daughter of a King, sometimes it was hard to convince my heart of that mind-boggling reality.

Have you ever struggled with the same feelings I felt? Even though your leaders have taught you about your divine heritage, has this truth ever been a little hard to swallow? Have you ever looked in the mirror and thought, *A princess? No way, that's not me.* If so, you might be relieved to hear that there's a reason you've been feeling that way. It's because there's much more to your story than just the part about you being a princess.

You see, even though you used to live in a celestial mansion with your heavenly parents, that part only represents the *first scene* of your story. A lot has happened to you since you left your heavenly home, so what we need to do now is look at the rest of the tale. We need to uncover all the *other* things you've experienced since you left those royal courts on high.

Perhaps you're thinking, *Yes, I know how the story goes. I know that when the time was right, I left my premortal life as a royal princess*

and came to earth to obtain a physical body. While that's definitely true and important to understand, would you be surprised if I told you, that still doesn't capture the whole story? If the truth be told, something shocking and dangerous happened to you when you came to earth—something that rocked your entire world. To make matters worse, you may not even know it happened.

We'll talk a lot more about these dangerous circumstances as we go along, but for now, let me give you a quick glimpse of what we're dealing with. Below I've listed four different verses from the scriptures—verses that may seem a little perplexing. As you read through each one, pay close attention to the emphasized word repeated in each verse. If it's okay, I'm going to add the feminine counterparts so the words sound more personal as you read them.

3 Nephi 9:17   As many as have received me, to them have I given to *become* the sons [and daughters] of God.

D&C 11:30   As many as receive me, to them will I give power to *become* the sons [and daughters] of God.

D&C 35:2   As many as will believe on my name . . . may *become* the sons [and daughters] of God.

D&C 45:8   Unto as many as received me gave I power . . . to *become* the sons [and daughters] of God.

Before we go any further, I want to remind you that the word *become* means to "change, or grow to be" something.[8] So these verses are telling us how we can "change" into or "grow to be" children of God. Don't you think that's a strange thing for the scriptures to say? I mean, didn't we just spend this whole chapter talking about how we *already are* daughters of God? Didn't we learn that important truth from President Uchtdorf, the Young Women theme, the *For the Strength of Youth* pamphlet, and the Personal Progress book? So why would the scriptures say we need to "become" something we already are? What in the world is going on with these verses?

Believe it or not, these scriptures are hinting at a great mystery—a mystery we're going to explore in the upcoming scenes of our story. Eventually we'll discover what happened to each of us when we came to earth and why we need to "become" a daughter of God once again. But the only way we can do that is by continuing on to the second scene of the story. It starts, surprisingly, with the entrance of another important character, one who's impacted your life more than you could ever imagine. (And I'll give you another hint: this character is *not* the handsome prince.)

For Additional Study

A great way for you to wrap up this first scene is by reading all of President Uchtdorf's talk "Your Happily Ever After." He gave it in the April 2010 Young Women broadcast. I know you'll love his story of how he met and courted his wife, and also his inspired counsel and relevant teachings. As you read, grab your journal and take notes of the things that stand out to you personally.

For those who have access to the Internet, I have an extra special treat. Deborah Owen, a Laurel from the Pacific Northwest, worked for over a year to make a video presentation that merges President Uchtdorf's talk with clips from several princess movies. It's absolutely wonderful and makes President Uchtdorf's work come alive in a whole new way. Here's the link if you'd like to watch it for yourself: bit.ly/happilyeveruchtdorf.

Before we move on, let's turn one more time to that little mystery we talked about at the end of that chapter—the mystery of our needing to "become" a daughter of God once again. Here are some additional scriptures you can read to study this idea in greater depth: John 1:12; Mosiah 27:25; Moroni 7:26, 48; D&C 34:3; Moses 6:68; 7:1. Make sure to write down any impressions that come to mind as you read.

A NOTORIOUS VILLAIN

PREPARE YOURSELF, BECAUSE our story is about to take a darker and more menacing turn. The evil villain is about to make his dramatic entrance. As you study this new character in the story, make sure not to base your mental picture of him on all those princess movies you've been watching. The villains in the animated films are definitely cunning and devious, but at times they can also be funny, witty, and even downright entertaining. Because they're animated characters, they often come across as perfectly harmless. But that's a mistake we can't afford to make in our own story. You see, unlike the movie versions, the villain in *your* princess story is very real and dangerous.

Here's how C. S. Lewis, author of *Mere Christianity*, describes this particular character:

> One of the things that surprised me when I first read the New Testament seriously was that it talked so much about a Dark Power in the universe—a mighty evil spirit who was held to be the Power behind death, disease, and sin. . . . Christianity thinks this Dark Power was created by God, and was good when he was created, and went wrong.[1]

What C. S. Lewis just said is true. The villain in your story *was* good when he was created; in fact, he was a royal prince in the same heavenly courts you used to live in. His name, as you probably know, is Lucifer. The Doctrine and Covenants tells us that in the premortal world, Lucifer was a "son of the morning" who "was in authority in the presence of God" (D&C 76:27, 25). What happened to make him lose that authority? Well, it all started when our Heavenly Father presented His glorious plan of happiness at the great council in heaven. As a part of that plan, Jesus Christ was chosen to be the Savior of the world, but Lucifer wanted that role (and all of God's glory and power) for himself. In other words, he wanted the starring role in the story, not just a small part. So he rebelled against our Father's plan and convinced a "third part of the hosts of heaven" to follow him (D&C 29:36).

As a result of his rebellion, our Father "caused that [Lucifer] should be cast down; and he became Satan, yea, even the devil, the father of all lies, to deceive and to blind men, and to lead them captive at his will, even as many as would not hearken unto [God's] voice" (Moses 4:3–4). Where was Satan cast down? Right here on earth with us. Because we're stuck in the same realm with him, it makes it much easier for him to use his scheming ways in tempting us to sin and ruin our lives. Rotten to the core, Satan "seeketh that all men might be miserable like unto himself" (2 Nephi 2:27).

Just like the princess character in our story, I'm sure you're familiar with the villain character as well. You've probably heard about the devil again and again throughout the years, not only from your parents and leaders but also from seminary teachers, prophets, and apostles. For example, in the priesthood session of the October 2011 general conference, Elder Jeffrey R. Holland highlighted two things about the adversary that he thought all LDS youth needed to understand:

> Number one, Satan, or Lucifer, or the father of lies—call him what you will—is real, the very personification of evil. His motives are in every case malicious, and he convulses at the appearance of redeeming light, at the very thought of truth. Number two, he is eternally opposed to the love of God, the Atonement of Jesus Christ, and the work of peace and salvation. He will fight against these whenever and wherever he can. He knows he will be defeated and cast out in the end, but he is determined to take down with him as many others as he possibly can.[2]

Elder Holland's words show us that, just like each movie princess, you too face an enemy who is mean, underhanded, and wicked. You too have an adversary who is manipulative, arrogant, and hateful. However, the difference between Satan and the animated villains is that you can't see Lucifer with your eyes or hear him with your ears, which makes it really easy to forget he's there. In fact, most of us go about our daily lives hardly giving the adversary a second thought. But in a story as riddled with danger as ours, that's something we can't afford to do. As Christian author John Eldredge warns,

> [Most people] don't take [evil] seriously. They don't live as though [their] story has a villain. Not the devil prancing around in red tights, carrying a pitchfork, *but the incarnation of the very worst of every enemy you've met in every other story.* . . .
>
> Life is very confusing if you do not take into account that there is a villain. That you, my friend, have an enemy.[3]

In order to understand your personal princess story, you must remember that you have an evil villain watching your every move, waiting for any opportunity to take you down. Just think about some of the horrible things the villains did to the princesses on the movie screen. Not one of those villains held back—and neither will Satan. Again and again, the scriptures reveal the lengths to which he'll go to lie to you, deceive you, and destroy your life. He'll stop at nothing to steal your happiness and make you miserable just like he is.

Several examples of this are found in the pages of the scriptures. In the Sacred Grove, the adversary seized Joseph Smith with his oppressive power and bound his tongue so that he couldn't speak (Joseph Smith—History 1:15). On the top of a mountain, Satan threw a temper tantrum when Moses refused to bow down and worship him as the Only Begotten (Moses 1:19). And in the wilderness of Judea, Lucifer tried three different times to tempt Jesus Christ Himself to sin against God (Luke 4:3–12). These stories prove that the villain in our story is not just sneaky but extremely evil. In the words of the Apostle Peter, he's "a roaring lion, [who] walketh about, seeking whom he may devour" (1 Peter 5:8).

To add to that, Lucifer has many servants waiting to help him accomplish his cruel and devious plans. As the Doctrine and Covenants tells us, a "third part of the hosts of heaven turned he away . . . because of their agency; and they were thrust down, and thus came the devil and his angels" (D&C 29:36–37). Think about that for a minute. A "third part of the hosts of heaven" are now the devil's angels. Call them sidekicks, accomplices, henchmen, or even his posse, their goal is to do all they can to support and sustain the purposes of their evil master.

I'm sure you've noticed that the villains in the princess movies always have a sidekick or two. That's just more evidence that our villain never works alone. As Elder Melvin J. Ballard warned,

> If our eyes were only opened to see the powers that are about us, that seek to influence us, we could not have the courage to walk alone and unassisted. These powers are about us, using their influence for the accomplishment of certain well-defined ends to win the coveted place for their chief, the fallen son of God . . . the devil.[4]

With that said, you may think your role as the princess is abundantly clear. As a daughter of the King, I'm sure you believe your goal is to resist Satan and his followers by choosing the right and keeping all of God's commandments. Because your role seems so obvious, you're probably confident that the villain will never get the best of you—that in the end, you'll see right through his conniving schemes and beat him at his own game. All I can say is, I wouldn't be too sure about that. There's something much bigger going on in our story, something that actually gives your enemy the upper hand. And it's something we'll talk about in the next scene.

For Additional Study

I'd again encourage you to read all of Elder Jeffrey R. Holland's talk "We Are All Enlisted" from the October 2011 general conference. I know it was given in the priesthood session, but Elder Holland got incredibly fired up when he gave this talk, and

I think young women need to hear it as much as young men (it's even better if you watch the actual video clip online).

The Bible Dictionary has a ton of information about the adversary under the heading "Devil." As you read through the entry, stop and look up any verses that seem especially intriguing to you. By studying more about the villain, it will help you understand exactly what kind of character you're dealing with in your personal princess story.

Finally, you may also want to read Elder Melvin J. Ballard's talk "Struggle for the Soul" from the March 1984 *New Era*. He does a great job painting the big picture of the villain's agenda to take us out any way he possibly can.

AN AWFUL MONSTER

I F YOU GREW up in the Church, I'm guessing you spent hundreds of hours of Primary and seminary and general conference being taught how to choose the right. And you probably read countless talks, lessons, and scriptures that outline the Lord's standards for righteous living. So you'd think it'd be easy to put all that information into practice. We all know what to do to resist the villain—so we just need to *do it*, right? The problem is, again and again, every single one of us has done just the opposite. We've yelled at a loved one or gossiped behind someone's back. We've disobeyed our parents or watched hours of TV while our scriptures gathered dust in the corner. Though we probably didn't mean to break God's commandments, we still did it anyway, even though we knew better.

After doing something sinful or stupid, have you ever asked yourself, "Why in the world did I do that? What's wrong with me? Why didn't I stop myself before it was too late?" I know I asked myself those questions while I was growing up. I really wanted to be good, but sometimes I just wasn't. Sometimes I made terrible choices and said awful things, even though I promised myself I would never act that way. It's like one day I acted like Beauty, and the next day I acted like the Beast.

This struggle reminds me of another popular princess movie we haven't mentioned yet. It's *Ella Enchanted*. Have you seen it?

It's a cute little fairy tale modeled loosely after the story of Cinderella. Like most princess movies, Ella marries the prince and becomes a princess in the end. But before that happens, she must overcome a difficult problem. You see, when Ella was a baby, a well-meaning but ditzy fairy godmother put her under a spell of obedience, but the spell turned out to be a curse rather than a blessing. It forced Ella to do everything anyone told her to do—even if it was mean, nasty, or downright impossible. Ella desperately wanted to break free from the spell, but for some reason she couldn't. Again and again, she continued to do things she knew were wicked and wrong.

As I watched this movie recently, one scene in particular really tugged on my heartstrings. It happened early in Ella's life when she had trouble understanding why she acted so strangely at times. In this scene, her mother and their household fairy finally sat Ella down and told her all about the obedience spell. When they finished, she looked up at her mom with pain in her big brown eyes and said, "I always knew something was wrong with me." In that moment, I knew exactly how Ella was feeling. So many times I've felt like something was wrong with me too. Even though I wanted to be good, it seemed like I always ended up blowing it in the end.

Now that I'm a mom of teenagers, I've watched my own children struggle with the same problem. I remember an experience with one of my daughters on a Sunday after she'd turned twelve and entered the Young Women program. That afternoon, she came to me with her Personal Progress book in hand and excitedly showed me the goal she'd chosen to work on for the next few weeks. It was the goal of trying to be a peacemaker in your home—trying to refrain from judging, criticizing, or speaking unkindly to other members of your family. I told her that sounded great and didn't think much more about it.

To my surprise, she came back just a few short hours later, only this time she had great big tears shining in her eyes. "Mom," she said, "I can't be a peacemaker. It's too hard." As we talked about it, she told me that every time she tried to be kind, one of her siblings did something to make her mad. So she'd take a deep breath and try harder, but the same thing would eventually happen all over again. She said the more she tried to be sweet, the more the angry feelings rose up inside her. I could tell, like Ella, she too was thinking, *I just know there is something wrong with me.*

Would it help to know that Nephi experienced the same feelings of discouragement and frustration? After what I'm guessing was a really bad day, he cried out, "O wretched man that I am! Yea, my heart sorroweth because of my flesh; my soul grieveth because of mine iniquities. I am encompassed about, because of the temptations and the sins which do so easily beset me" (2 Nephi 4:17–18).

Nephi's agony makes me wonder: Why is it so hard sometimes to choose the right? I mean, why can't we just tell ourselves to stop sinning—and then stop? I'd like to suggest there's a reason we have such a hard time being obedient. It's because, just like Ella, there *is* something wrong with us—something very wrong. But to understand it, we've got to dive into the third scene of our story. It's a scene that involves a dangerous monster, one so strong and powerful that it strikes fear in the hearts of even the bravest of men.

What? You're surprised to see a monster popping up in our princess story? You shouldn't be. Most princess stories have some sort of horrible creature who terrorizes the princess. Haven't you heard the tale of a fire-breathing dragon that swoops down, grabs the princess, and carries her off to his lair, where she must wait for the hero to come and rescue her? The scenario is so common that Wikipedia actually has an entry called "Princess and dragon." It explains all the different ways this story has been told and retold over the centuries in civilizations like ancient Greece, Russia, and Japan.[1]

Believe it or not, the theme of the princess and the dragon is also found in the Book of Mormon. If that sounds a little far-fetched, turn with me to the writings of Nephi's little brother Jacob in 2 Nephi 9 and check this out: "O how great the goodness of our God, who prepareth a way for our escape from the grasp of this awful monster; yea, that monster, death and hell, which I call the death of the body, and also the death of the spirit" (2 Nephi 9:10).

I hope you're ready, because this verse drops us headfirst into the third scene of our story. In this scene, you—the noble princess—have been taken captive by what Jacob calls an "awful monster." To help you visualize this part of the story, I want you to picture yourself standing in the middle of a peaceful meadow, dressed in a shimmering white gown. You could even envision delicate flowers in your hair and soft satin slippers on your feet.

Next, imagine a hideous dragon coming out of nowhere and scooping you up with its razor-sharp claws. Can you feel the heat of the dragon's fire-breath burning through the sleeves of your dress? Can you imagine the feel of its rough, jagged scales? I want you to pretend that, no matter how hard you struggle, kick, or beat on the dragon, you can't break free from its suffocating grip. You're trapped—held prisoner by a creature that fills your heart with overwhelming terror and dread.

Now, for the most shocking part of all. That scene you just created in your mind isn't make-believe or pretend. It describes exactly what happened to *you*, royal princess, after you came to earth. You were taken captive by a terrible monster, and this beast plans on keeping you locked up for the rest of eternity. I know you may be saying, "What are you talking about? I'm not trapped in the grip of a terrible monster." If you'll just stay with me, the rest of the scene will soon make more sense.

To see this monster in our lives, we have to start by reviewing the story of Adam and Eve. We know from the scriptures that after God created the world, He placed Adam and Eve in the Garden of Eden. And at that time, He "gave unto them commandments that they should love and serve him, the only living and true God, and that he should be the only being whom they should worship" (D&C 20:19). He also introduced the couple to the tree of knowledge of good and evil and told them that they would die if they chose to partake of that particular fruit (Moses 3:17).

Of course, it wasn't long before the villain showed up in the Garden and "put it into the heart of [a] serpent" to tempt Eve to eat from the forbidden tree (Moses 4:6). To make a long story short, both she and Adam took a big bite of the fruit, and the consequence of their choice didn't just affect the two of them. It had rippling effects that would impact every single one of us who would ever live on the earth. What was that consequence? It's described with two simple words: *the Fall.*

The Bible Dictionary gives us this information about the Fall:

> The fall of Adam and Eve is one of the most important occurrences in the history of man. . . . With the eating of the "forbidden fruit," Adam and Eve became mortal, sin entered, and death became a part of life. . . . After Adam fell, the whole creation fell and became mortal. *Adam's Fall brought both physical and spiritual death into the world upon all mankind.*[2]

So, according to the Bible Dictionary (and also scriptures like Alma 42:9 and Helaman 14:16), the Fall brought *physical* and *spiritual* death—not just upon Adam and Eve but upon "all mankind." Surprisingly, that ties in perfectly with what Jacob said about the awful monster. If you look back at Jacob's verse, you'll see that the prophet described the monster like this: "Yea, that monster, death and hell, which I call the death of the body, and also the death of the spirit." Did you notice that Jacob's dragon represented *two* things, not just one? In other words, it's a two-headed dragon holding us in its clutches. In order to better understand this horrible creature, let's talk about the two different heads one at a time.

As we picture the first head of the monster, I think it would help to give it a name. The name Jacob chose for the first head was "the death of the body." This is the "physical death" that the Bible Dictionary was talking about. So I want you to imagine the words *Death of the Body* scrawled across one of the dragon's scaly foreheads. With that image in mind, here's the question I want you to ponder: How does "the death of the body" hold you tightly in its grasp? It's probably an easy one to answer. After all, isn't every single one of us going to die someday? It's something we can't escape, no matter how much we may want to. Even if we fight and scream and struggle against this dragon called death, we'll never be able to break free from its powerful grip.

Unfortunately, there's even more to this head of the dragon. Physical death involves much more than just laying our body in the grave someday. It also means that while we're here on earth, we're stuck in a mortal body, not an immortal one like our Father in Heaven. And being mortal means our body will get sick or injured from time to time. It means we'll feel weak, exhausted, or even overcome with pain. It may even mean we'll be afflicted with a disease where our muscles don't work right or our brain doesn't function the way it should. To sum up, because of the Fall, things will happen to our body that we won't like and won't be able to control. It's not a fun state to be trapped in.

To add to that, Jacob reveals that without the plan of salvation, this terrible monster would hold us captive for the rest of eternity. Once we die, our death would be permanent, meaning it would last forever and ever. Here's how Jacob put it: "Wherefore, the first judgment which came upon man *must needs have remained to an endless duration. And if so, this flesh must have laid down to rot and to crumble to its mother earth, to rise no more*" (2 Nephi 9:7; emphasis added). Not a very happy ending for a royal princess, is it?

Can you see yourself—a royal daughter of God—trapped in the grasp of this awful monster? Can you feel the strength of its claws and picture its piercing yellow eyes? Are you imagining the words *Death of the Body* etched into one of its giant heads? I hope so, because now it's time to move to the second head of the monster. And I'll warn you that this second head is even more dangerous than the first. In the words of President Joseph F. Smith, it's "a more terrible death than that of the body."[3]

So how did Jacob describe the second head of the dragon? He called it "the death of the spirit." It's the other kind of death mentioned in the Bible Dictionary. I want you to think about this particular death for a minute. Here Jacob is talking about our *spirit* dying, not just our body. Have you ever considered the fact that because of the Fall, your spirit also experienced its own kind of death? It's a strange idea to contemplate. You may wonder how your spirit can be dead if you're still breathing, talking, and walking around. I mean, isn't your spirit what gives life to your body? For most of us, the death of our spirit is a really confusing thing to figure out.

I think it will help if we turn to the scriptures to learn what Jacob meant by "the death of the spirit." Thankfully, Jacob wasn't the only one who talked about this head of the monster. Nephi, Alma, and Samuel the Lamanite all mentioned it too, only they took the phrase "death of the spirit" and turned it around to "spiritual death" (see 2 Nephi 9:12; Alma 12:16; 42:9; Helaman 14:16–18). So when you picture the second head of the dragon, I want you to picture in huge writing on its head *Death of the Spirit* or *Spiritual Death*.

Now we need to figure out what causes each of us to die spiritually. How in the world do we get trapped in the clutches of this monster? There's only one way. The Lord explained it in the Doctrine and Covenants by using the example of what happened to Adam when he ate the forbidden fruit:

> Wherefore, it came to pass that the devil tempted Adam, and *he partook of the forbidden fruit and transgressed the commandment,* wherein he became subject to the will of the devil, because he yielded unto temptation.
>
> Wherefore, I, the Lord God, caused that he should be cast out from the Garden of Eden, from my presence, *because of his transgression, wherein he became spiritually dead.* (D&C 29:40–41; emphasis added)

In these verses, we learn what not only happened to Adam but also happens to each of us when we break God's commandments. When we partake of forbidden fruit (meaning Satan tempts us, and we make the choice to sin), the punishment for our sin is spiritual death. And because every single one of us has sinned, we're all caught in the grasp of spiritual death.

To prove my point, listen to the words of Samuel the Lamanite: "*All* mankind, by the fall of Adam, . . . are considered as dead, both as to things temporal and to things spiritual" (Helaman 14:16). In our day, Elder Dallin H. Oaks has also made it clear that "since 'all have sinned,' we are *all* spiritually dead."[4] I think it's one of the scariest parts of our personal princess story—and also one of the most misunderstood.

For instance, I remember having a discussion with a class of thirteen-year-olds about the two-headed monster holding us in its grip. I was teaching their Sunday School lesson, and I asked the kids to raise their hands if they thought they were spiritually dead. To my surprise, not one of the youth held up a hand. Eventually, I realized the class thought spiritual death was something that *might* happen to them someday if they committed some really big sin. They had no idea that the small sins they'd already committed were enough to cause them to die spiritually.

If nothing else, what I hope you learn in this scene of the story is that spiritual death isn't just something that affects really bad or wicked people. Instead, it's a monster that holds every single one of us in its rock-solid grip. That includes the kids who walk down the hallways at school, the lady who helps you in the store at the mall, and the celebrities who pose on the red carpet. It even includes the men and women in the scriptures. Because of the Fall, "*all* mankind [are] in a lost and in a fallen state" (1 Nephi 10:6; emphasis added). It's not an easy scene to talk about in our personal princess story.

The good news is, once we understand that we're trapped in the clutches of the monster of physical and spiritual death, we can finally move to the next scene in our story. What comes next? Well, we need to talk about what actually happens to us when we die spiritually. After all, most of us understand what happens with the death of our body since we're used to experiencing pain, exhaustion, weakness, illness, and injury. And we've probably known someone who's died as well. But it's a lot harder to comprehend the death of our spirit because it happens on the inside of us rather than the outside.

Pay close attention as we go through the next scene, because the plot is about to get a lot more complicated.

For Additional Study

If you'll turn to the Topical Guide, you'll find many verses about the Fall under the heading "Man, Natural, Not Spiritually Reborn." When you have some extra time, read through that

section and look up any scriptures that stand out to you. You can also do the same thing with the heading "Fall of Man."

Next, turn to 2 Nephi 9 and spend some time reading and pondering the entire chapter. Can you feel Jacob's anxiety over what happened to us because of the Fall? You may even want to count the number of exclamation points he uses. Jacob was definitely a passionate prophet—one who tried hard to help us understand how far we've fallen and why we so desperately need a Savior and Redeemer.

Elder Jeffrey R. Holland posed an incredibly haunting question in his April 2015 general conference talk, "Where Justice, Love, and Mercy Meet." Speaking of the Fall, he said,

> What a plight! The entire human race in free fall—every man, woman, and child in it physically tumbling toward permanent death, spiritually plunging toward eternal anguish. Is that what life was meant to be? Is this the grand finale of the human experience?[5]

(You'll have to read the rest of his talk to find the wonderful answer to that difficult question.)

A DRAGON NATURE

I THINK ONE OF the coolest series ever written is The Chronicles of Narnia by C. S. Lewis. If you want stories about princes and princesses, evil villains, and heroic rescues, you'll find it all right there. I especially love the fourth book, *The Voyage of the Dawn Treader*, because in its pages, Lewis uses an analogy that perfectly captures what happens to each of us as a result of the Fall. Because the film version doesn't illustrate this particular analogy very well, I'm going to tell you Eustace's story exactly as C. S. Lewis tells it in the book. I believe this little tale will help us understand exactly what happens when we sin and become captive to the monster of spiritual death.

If you've read the book (or seen the movie), you know about Eustace, the obnoxious cousin of the Pevensies who accidentally traveled to Narnia with Edmund and Lucy. When they arrived, the three found themselves on a ship called the *Dawn Treader*. Eustace hated being on the ship, so when the *Dawn Treader* docked on an island, Eustace knew his chance had come to get away. Quickly, he snuck off the boat and set out to explore the fascinating new land. Before long, the boy actually stumbled on a dragon's lair. Once he learned the dragon that lived there had died, he crept into the cave and gloried in all the riches the creature had accumulated. Worn out from all the excitement, he curled up on the dragon's fortune and fell asleep.

When Eustace awoke, he saw a thin trail of smoke, a pair of sharp claws, and a long, scaly tail. Terrified, Eustace concluded that a dragon must have returned to the cave while he was sleeping. But then he noticed something odd: the dragon claws wiggled when he wiggled his fingers, and the dragon breath went in and out to the same rhythm as his own breath. Rushing out of the cave, Eustace ran to a nearby pool and searched for his reflection in the water. C. S. Lewis described what happened next:

> In an instant he realized the truth. The dragon face in the pool was his own reflection. There was no doubt of it. It moved as he moved: it opened and shut its mouth as he opened and shut his.
>
> He had turned into a dragon while he was asleep. Sleeping on a dragon's hoard with greedy, dragonish thoughts in his heart, *he had become a dragon himself.*[1]

At first, Eustace thought it was fun being a dragon, especially when he learned that he could breathe fire and fly all over the island. However, as the days turned into weeks, the novelty wore off and he desperately wanted to return to his life as a boy. But no matter how hard he tried, he just couldn't change back into his old self. Eustace fell into despair, for "it was very dreary being a dragon."[2]

Let's pause at this point, because we need to talk about how Eustace's experience applies to each of us. (I promise we'll finish the rest of the story later.) In order to get the most out of C. S. Lewis's analogy, I want you to go back to that scene in your imagination where the monster is holding you captive. Picture again your flowing white dress, the flowers tucked in your hair, and the dragon's beefy claws locked tightly around your middle. Now imagine the dragon spreading its wings and taking flight with you still held firmly in its clutches. As the cold wind rushes your face, your eyes begin to water, and you wonder where the creature is taking you. You squirm in its grasp as your feet dangle over leafy treetops and jagged mountain peaks. Finally, the monster lands with a thud in front of what looks like the entrance of a dingy, foul-smelling cave.

Your heart sinks as the dragon pulls you inside the lair and tosses you roughly to the ground. However, your fear quickly turns to astonishment as a shocking sight unfolds before your eyes. Milling around the cave are hundreds of dragons, all different shapes and sizes. Big ones, small ones, round ones, tall ones—there are dragons everywhere you look. You huddle against the wall and try to blend in. All of a sudden, something even more shocking begins to happen. The skin on your body slowly starts turning a horrible shade of greenish-gray. Next, scales form on your arms and legs, and claws grow in place of your toes. You lift your hands to your face only to find that your fingers are forming into claws as well. At that moment, the awful reality hits you: You weren't just taken captive by a dragon. You've *become* a dragon yourself.

Freeze that scene in your mind for a minute, and let's see how it fits into our personal princess story. I know that, again, you're probably thinking this scene is completely imaginary or that I'm trying to make the story scarier or more dramatic for the sake of entertainment. Unfortunately, that's not the case. Just like the previous parts of our princess story, this scenario is also very real. You, noble princess, have turned into a dragon. If you don't believe me, let me read you a few verses from the Book of Mormon.

For starters, listen to Alma's explanation of what happened to all of us as a result of the Fall: "The fall had brought upon all mankind a spiritual death as well as a temporal, that is, they were cut off from the presence of the Lord. . . . Therefore, . . . they had become *carnal, sensual, and devilish, by nature*"(Alma 42:9–10; emphasis added).

Think about that last phrase for a minute. Alma said our "nature" has become "*carnal, sensual,* and *devilish*" as a result of the Fall. King Benjamin taught the same thing, only his version is a lot shorter: "In Adam, or *by nature, [we] fall*" (Mosiah 3:16; emphasis added.). To add to that, the brother of Jared pointed out that "because of the fall *our natures* have become *evil continually*" (Ether 3:2; emphasis added).

Did you notice that all three of those prophets said something serious happened to our *nature* when we fell? I know you've heard that word a lot in the Church, especially in the Young Women program. But have you ever thought much about what it means? What is your nature, exactly? How would you define it? One way to look at our nature is as our "inborn or inherent qualities" or our "disposition or temperament."[3] Our nature can also be described as our personality, our essence, or our character.[4] To sum up, our nature is who we are on the inside—who we are deep in our heart.

So if we take that definition and plug it into the Book of Mormon verses we just read, we hear Alma saying that because of our spiritual death, our personality or character has become carnal, sensual, and devilish. We hear King Benjamin saying that our character is now fallen. And we hear the brother of Jared saying that, deep inside, our disposition and temperament has become evil continually. Those are some pretty troubling teachings, don't you think? In fact, they may not seem like they apply to you and me at all.

You may even be thinking, *Wait just one minute. This isn't part of my story. I'm not carnal, sensual, or devilish. My nature isn't "evil continually." I try to choose the right and keep the commandments, so there's no way those verses are talking about me. Those prophets must be referring to someone else.* I wouldn't blame you if you had those kinds of thoughts and feelings. This doctrine can be a really difficult one to understand.

First of all, let me just say that I know a lot of young women in the Church who try hard to walk the straight and narrow path. If that describes you, you may be reviewing your actions and thinking, *I'm a good person. I go to church. I don't smoke or drink or do drugs. I attend seminary and read my scriptures. I don't watch R-rated movies, dress immodestly, or hang around people who swear. Isn't that proof that my nature isn't carnal, sensual, and devilish? That I have a divine nature rather than an evil one like the brother of Jared said?*

Let's answer that by taking a closer look at the phrase *divine nature*. We already said that our nature is our personality, disposition, or temperament, right? So next we need to define the word *divine*. *Divine* means "godlike" or "characteristic of or befitting a deity."[5] Having a "divine nature," then, means having a personality or temperament just like Jesus Christ or our Father in

Heaven. Those with a "divine nature" act as They would act, think as They would think, and feel as They would feel—at all times, in all things, and in all places.

Now think about your own nature, about all the thoughts, feelings, and actions you display on a daily basis. Tell me: Can you honestly place your nature side by side with God's and say you think, feel, and act exactly like Him? That your character is just like His? That your temperament and personality resemble His in every way? I know you may have made some righteous choices over the years, but even with that good track record, can you really say that your nature—the deepest part of you—is *divine*? That you are *godlike* in everything you do and say?

Neither can I.

Here's the difficult truth we learn in this scene of the princess story: when we died spiritually, each of us turned into a dragon—or what King Benjamin likes to call a "natural man" (Mosiah 3:19). And like Alma said, our natural man is carnal, sensual, and devilish *by nature*. To put that in modern language, it simply means that most of the time, we're more drawn to a shopping trip, a TV show, or a pint of ice cream than to the things of God. It means that social media is way more fun than Sunday School and that texting is cooler than working on family history. It means we can be selfish, disobedient, and impatient, and we have a devilish tendency to follow our own will rather than the will of the Lord.

To make this a little more personal, join me in taking a short little quiz. Don't worry—it's only ten questions to help you see what happened to your nature because of the Fall. Since no one will see the answers but you, I want you to be completely honest with yourself as you read through the following questions:

Have you ever lied to a friend, a parent, or a teacher—even a little white lie that no one else knows about?

Have you ever gossiped about someone or judged them based on their outward appearance?

Do you ever spend more time and attention on things of the world (Internet, movies, television, new clothes) than things of the Lord?

Have you ever been unkind, meaning you've passed by someone who needed help or failed to stand up for someone who was being ridiculed?

Have you ever bragged about yourself or tried to make yourself more popular in the eyes of your peers?

Have you ever disobeyed your parents or maintained a rebellious attitude against them in your heart and mind?

Have you ever yelled at, insulted, or fought with someone, especially a member of your family?

Have you ever held a grudge or refused to forgive someone who hurt you?

Have you ever been guilty of idleness, laziness, or procrastination?

Have you ever entertained inappropriate thoughts that were impure, selfish, or sinful?

I'm guessing that, like me, you had to answer yes to most of those questions. Please understand, I didn't give you that quiz to make you feel guilty, ashamed, or embarrassed in any way. I did it so you could see that even though you may be doing a lot of good things on the outside (like going to church, paying tithing, reading scriptures, and performing service with your ward), still, something changed in your heart when you died spiritually. As a result, your nature is now more dragon-like than Christlike, meaning you continue to say, do, and feel things that are sinful and wrong. That's what happens when a person is held captive by the monster of spiritual death.

Obviously, spiritual death is not a fun state to be trapped in. In fact, it's pretty awful. Listen to the way President Joseph F. Smith described what happened to Adam when he went through his own spiritual death:

> Yet living, he was dead—dead to God, dead to light and truth, dead spiritually; cast out from the presence of God. . . . He was within the grasp of Satan. . . . He was 'spiritually dead'—banished from the presence of God. And if there had not been a way of escape provided for him, his death would have been a perpetual, endless, eternal death, without any hope of redemption.[6]

Right there we learn what it's like to be spiritually dead. It means we've been "cast out" or "banished" from our Father's presence like President Smith just said. And that banishment can bring with it some pretty negative thoughts and emotions. It's the reason you feel hopeless, helpless, or alone sometimes. It's the reason you feel down, discouraged, or depressed. I bet you blamed those awful feelings on your stressful life, didn't you? Or maybe you blamed them on family issues, friend problems, or that crazy teacher who gave you too much homework. Well, now you know that many of the negative feelings we experience often come as a result of our dragon nature. Just like physical death causes us physical pain, spiritual death causes emotional pain to stir inside our heart. Like Eustace said, it's dreary being a dragon.

As hard as that may have been to hear, I want you to prepare yourself, because President Smith also revealed more bad news in this scene of our story. Did you notice how he said that spiritual death put Adam "within the grasp of Satan"? Were you at all curious what he meant by that? To find out what the prophet was talking about, we need to go back into the pages of the scriptures.

If we return to the same chapter we've been studying, we'll see that Jacob said once we're in the grasp of the awful monster, we "become *subject* to that angel who fell from before the presence of God" (2 Nephi 9:8; emphasis added). And we already learned in the Doctrine and Covenants that when Adam "partook of the forbidden fruit and transgressed the commandment, . . . he became *subject* to the will of the devil" (D&C 29:40; emphasis added). Now for the worst part of all: the word *subject* actually means "being under domination, control, or influence."[7] Add that to the scriptures above and we learn that when we made the choice to sin, we became *subject* not just to the two-headed monster but to *Satan*

himself. In other words, the Fall gave the villain power to take us captive. We are now in his clutches and under his command.

To illustrate, return with me one more time to that mental scene you created in the dragon's lair. Picture again how it feels to be stuck in the cave with all the other captives who have also turned into dragons. Now imagine that you're searching every inch of the lair to find a way out when suddenly you come face to face with the evil villain himself. Cackling at the fear in your eyes, he leans in and coldly whispers, "You're mine now. You can never escape. You're my prisoner for the rest of eternity." Finally you realize you're not in a dragon's cave at all—you're trapped in the dungeon of the most horrible villain who has ever existed.

If you're having a hard time believing this imaginary scene is real, listen to the haunting words of Abinadi in the Book of Mormon. He says that as long as we "[remain] in [our] fallen state . . . *the devil hath all power over [us]*" (Mosiah 16:5; emphasis added). And Jacob tells us that, left in this state, our destiny is to "become devils, angels to a devil, to be shut out from the presence of our God, and to remain with the father of lies, in misery" forever (2 Nephi 9:9). It's an incredibly disturbing issue. And it just shows yet again that you, noble princess, have been taken prisoner by a wicked villain, and he has no intention of ever letting you go.

Now, I know there's a chance you're one of those strong-minded people who's thinking, "No way—I'm not going to be anyone's prisoner. I'm getting out of the lair as fast as I can." All I can say is, good luck with that, because no matter how much you struggle and strain, you're not going to be able to break free from your stubborn natural man.

Eustace learned that lesson when he was trying to change himself from a dragon back into a boy. Look at to what happened when he tried to take off his dragon skin so he could bathe in a pool of cool spring water:

> I started scratching myself and my scales began coming off all over the place. And then I scratched a little deeper and, instead of just scales coming off here and there, my whole skin started peeling off beautifully . . . as if I was a banana. In a minute or two, I just stepped out of it. I could see it lying there beside me, looking

rather nasty. It was a most lovely feeling. So I started to go down into the well for my [bath].

But just as I was going to put my feet into the water I looked down and saw that they were all hard and rough and wrinkled and scaly just as they had been before. Oh, that's all right, said I, it only means I had another smaller suit on underneath the first one, and I'll have to get out of it too. So I scratched and tore again and this underskin peeled off beautifully and out I stepped and left it lying beside the other one and went down to the well for my [bath].

Well, exactly the same thing happened again. And I thought to myself, oh dear, how ever many skins have I got to take off? . . . So I scratched away for the third time and got off a third skin, just like the two others, and stepped out of it. But as soon as I looked at myself in the water I knew it had been no good.[8]

I'm guessing the same thing has happened to you a time or two. Maybe you noticed it when you were trying to get rid of one of your sinful habits—like a bad temper. Perhaps you were able to peel off that part of your natural man for a little while, but eventually you ended up yelling at your brother or sister even though you said you'd never do it ever again. Or maybe you tried really hard to read your scriptures every night, but then you forgot all about them for a couple of weeks. Or it could be that you lied or talked behind someone's back or watched something you shouldn't have watched, even though you'd repented and promised the Lord that you were going to stop doing that particular sin. It's something we've all experienced at one time or another. Again and again we've tried to scratch off the bad habits and sins of our natural man, but just like Eustace, our sinful nature keeps coming back, even when we think we've gotten rid of it.

Unfortunately, that brings us to the most distressing news of our entire princess story. Because we've turned into dragons who continue to give in to the temptation of sin, we've become *enemies* to our precious Father in Heaven. If you don't believe me, consider King Benjamin's familiar words: "For the natural man is an *enemy to God*, and has been from the fall of Adam" (Mosiah 3:19; emphasis added). I hate to say it, but that includes you, royal princess.

As I was doing research for this book, I discovered an image that perfectly captures everything we've been talking about. It was a picture of the Disney princesses posing together, only this version was unlike any I'd ever seen. Each and every princess was *dressed in the outfit of her villain*. I'm not kidding. It was a really troubling image. (If you want to see if for yourself, just Google "Disney princesses as villains.") This portrait paints the exact picture of our predicament while in mortality. Our spiritual death has changed each of us from a princess into an enemy of God—one who often thinks and acts more like a villain than a daughter of royalty.

Perhaps now you can see why the scriptures say we must "become" a daughter of God once again. It's because we're not who we used to be. Each of us has developed a dragon nature (or natural man), and we must be changed and transformed before we can return to our Father's celestial mansion. The prophet Alma puts it like this: "Marvel not that *all mankind*, yea, men and women, all nations, kindreds, tongues and people, must be born again; yea, born of God, *changed from their carnal and fallen state, to a state of righteousness*, being redeemed of God, *becoming his sons and daughters*" (Mosiah 27:25; emphasis added).

There it is again. We must *become* a daughter of God by being changed from our "carnal and fallen state, to a state of righteousness." The confusing part is knowing *how* that important change will take place. Yes, we need to be converted from dragons back into royal princesses, but we've already talked about how we can't change ourselves back on our own. Our dragon nature just keeps coming back again and again, no matter how many times we try to peel it off. So what in the world is a fallen princess to do?

If things seem bleak and hopeless at this point, don't worry, because our story is about to take a miraculous turn. Though we've faced a lot of bad news in the last few scenes, the good news is that you're about to meet the most important character of all. You guessed it. It's finally time for the entrance of the handsome prince.

For Additional Study

Here are some verses where prophets and apostles speak clearly about the effects of the Fall on their own lives and those of their people: 2 Nephi 1:15; Mosiah 4:5–11; Mosiah 23:11; Alma 26:12; 42:7–15; Romans 7 (this last one is a lot easier to read if you go to the Joseph Smith Translation in the Appendix). If even the prophets and apostles struggled with the consequences of the Fall, what does that teach you about your personal life?

In 1 Corinthians 2:14, Paul talks about one particular characteristic of our natural man. Read through this verse (and the footnotes) and try to see how this could apply to your own life.

I think Moses 6:55 is an interesting scripture. Look it up and see what Moses says happens to children as they grow up (notice especially what happens to their *hearts*). Do you believe this is true? Is there anything in your life that would show it's true for you personally?

Now turn to Ephesians 4:22. Paul speaks of the natural man (he actually calls it "the old man") and describes it with one specific phrase. To better understand Paul's meaning, look up the words *corrupt*, *deceitful*, and *lust*. Can you think of any ways this verse could apply to your own natural man?

AN AWE-INSPIRING HERO

Heroic music, please. It's the moment we've all been waiting for—the moment when we finally get to meet our Prince Charming. Like all princes, he'll arrive just in time to save the day. It's a scene found in countless princess stories, and I'm not just talking about the animated movies either. Almost every princess has a prince who comes to her rescue. In *Star Wars*, Luke Skywalker sneaks onto the Death Star and frees Princess Leah from the clutches of Darth Vader. And in *The Princess Bride*, Westley storms the castle and saves Princess Buttercup from the awful Humperdinck. Like we said earlier, a princess story just wouldn't be a princess story without a handsome prince.

What I love about the prince is that he always seems to appear at the moment when things are at their most perilous—when it looks like the story can never, ever have a happy ending. That's when he bursts on the scene, sweeps the princess into his arms, and destroys the villain in one fell swoop. It's a scene I know you've read about in books and watched on TV. Well, now it's time for the prince to jump off the TV screen and right into your personal life. And believe me when I tell you that he's everything you've always hoped your Prince Charming would be.

Unfortunately, the princess movies get it totally wrong when it comes to the part of the prince. That's because the prince in your story isn't your future husband. In fact, your prince isn't even

mortal. A mortal man wouldn't have enough power to save you from the awful monster of physical and spiritual death, and a mortal man wouldn't be able to conquer the villain lurking in the unseen realm either. No, what you need is a prince with *supernatural power*. In the end, that's the only thing strong enough to free you from the monster's iron-like grip.

The hero you're about to meet is truly a man of no small reputation. His bravery is so spectacular, endless books have been written about Him over the centuries. His love is so consuming, thousands of songs have been penned to praise His name. His power is so miraculous, He's been called Savior, Deliverer, the Mighty One of Israel, and the Lion of the tribe of Judah (1 Nephi 22:12; D&C 138:23; Revelation 5:5). His name is known far and wide by billions of people all over the earth. That name, as I'm sure you've already guessed, is Jesus Christ.

Jesus actually took His place in our story a long time ago in premortal life. And when He assumed the role of the Prince, He inherited an incredibly difficult responsibility. As our Savior, He would have to leave His Father's castle and venture straight into enemy territory in order to save us. Notice that our Prince didn't send His servants to try and rescue us—He came for us *Himself*. However, once He arrived in the dragon's lair, He did something strange, something that didn't make sense to any of the captives who were waiting to be rescued. He allowed the villain's servants to capture him and kill him. Many people wondered why He gave Himself up so easily. At the time, it must have seemed like a horrible decision, like a tragic ending that could never be undone.

But our Prince understood something we often forget. He couldn't just charge into the dragon's lair and steal us away from the villain. That would be like breaking someone out of prison. It wouldn't rid us of the charges against us or erase the guilty plea hanging over our heads.

What charges, you ask? Remember, we've already talked about the punishment we've received for our sins—physical and spiritual death. Unfortunately, that consequence wasn't just for a limited time, like a mom putting her two-year-old in time out. As Jacob said, "The first judgment which came upon man must needs have remained *to an endless duration*" (2 Nephi 9:7). That means there would never be a moment when our Heavenly Father would say, "Okay, you've suffered enough. You can come back home." No, our sentence was permanent—and Jesus knew it. Like Abinadi, He knew that "all mankind were lost; and . . . they would have been *endlessly lost* were it not that God redeemed his people from their lost and fallen state" (Mosiah 16:4; emphasis added).

So our Prince's only option was to "redeem" us from our bondage like Abinadi just said. Now, I know you've probably heard Jesus called your Redeemer in hymns, lessons, and general conference talks. The word is also mentioned over two hundred times in the scriptures. But have you ever thought about what it actually means? If we go back to Dictionary.com, we'll learn that *redeem* means "to buy back."[1] In other words, Jesus "bought [us] with a price" when He redeemed us from the dragon's lair (1 Corinthians 6:20). It's just like in the movies when a criminal is holding someone hostage and he'll only let that person go if a rich man pays a huge sum of money as a ransom. In our story, though, we need to remember that *we* are the hostages and Jesus is the rich man who paid the ransom to set us free.

So what price did our Savior pay to buy our freedom? The Apostle Peter makes it excruciatingly clear: "[We] were not redeemed with . . . silver and gold . . . but with the precious blood of Christ" (1 Peter 1:18–19). In other words, our Prince "gave *himself* [as] a ransom for all" (1 Timothy 2:6; emphasis added). Tell me, could there be any greater love than that—for the Prince to give *His life* as a ransom so we could be released from captivity? It truly is the greatest love story that's ever been told.

It reminds me of what Eugene did for Rapunzel at the end of the movie Tangled. In the final moments of the story, he cut off Rapunzel's magical hair even though he could have used its power to save his life. In short, he loved Rapunzel so much that he was willing to die so she could be free from Gothel's evil influence. And that's how much your Redeemer loves you too. In fact, Jesus's love for you is so deep that He was willing to look the villain straight in the eye and say, "Take me instead. Give *me* the princess's punishment so she can go free." It's the reason He let

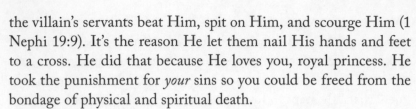

the villain's servants beat Him, spit on Him, and scourge Him (1 Nephi 19:9). It's the reason He let them nail His hands and feet to a cross. He did that because He loves you, royal princess. He took the punishment for *your* sins so you could be freed from the bondage of physical and spiritual death.

As hard as it may be to imagine our beloved Prince dying such a horrible death, let's not forget, that awful scene wasn't the end of the story. Once the Prince breathed His last breath, the stage was set for the most mind-blowing event in all of history. Yes, for a few hours, the earth shook and lightning split the brooding sky (3 Nephi 8:6–7). And, yes, for a few hours, Jesus's servants thought all was lost and the story had a tragic ending. But just when things were darkest, something absolutely astonishing happened: Jesus's battered and broken body came back to life.

While we don't know exactly how it happened, I like to imagine that God's radiant light and power entered our Prince's body through the tips of His toes and traveled slowly up the length of His frame, renewing, healing, and restoring Jesus—not back to His former condition but to a completely perfected and resurrected state. Through this process, our Prince became much more than a hero; He became an "Eternal God" just like His Heavenly Father (2 Nephi 26:12). Through His courageous Atonement and Resurrection, our Deliverer "[broke] the bands of death [so] that the grave"—and the enemy—would have "no victory" over us (Mosiah 16:7). I think that makes Him the most awe-inspiring hero ever to walk the earth.

I know you may be thinking, *Yes, I already know all about the Prince. I learned about Him in Primary, family home evening, and Sunday School. I've heard prophets and apostles speak about Him in general conference. I've even read poems about Him and hung pictures of Him on my bedroom wall. So that must mean I've been saved by Him—that I'm no longer a prisoner in the dragon's lair.* If such thoughts crossed your mind, let me make one thing crystal clear: even if you know a lot about the handsome Prince and even if you believe in Him, that doesn't necessarily mean you've been rescued or saved from the dragon's lair.

Take Cinderella, for instance. We all know she had her big moment at the ball, where she got to meet and even dance with Prince Charming. It was definitely a breathtaking and incredible night. But once the clock struck twelve, where did she end up? Right back in the hands of her evil stepmother. Other movie princesses faced a similar situation. Obviously, just meeting and getting to know their hero wasn't enough. Much more needed to happen before each princess could live happily ever after with her prince. And the same thing is true in your personal princess story.

Thankfully, your Prince already knows exactly how He's going to rescue you. He has a strategy all figured out. If you grew up in the Church, I'm sure you've heard about His plan. It's called the *gospel*, which is a word that simply means "good news."[2] (I actually think it's more like *great* news or *amazing* news or *absolutely miraculous* news. But that's just me.) So what is this incredible plan found in the gospel of Jesus Christ? It's summed up beautifully in the fourth article of faith:

> We believe that the first principles and ordinances of the Gospel are: first, Faith in the Lord Jesus Christ; second, Repentance; third, Baptism by immersion for the remission of sins; fourth, Laying on of hands for the gift of the Holy Ghost. (Articles of Faith 1:4)

That, in a nutshell, is the Prince's plan to rescue you. So the first step is having faith, right? Not exactly. Plain old faith will never be enough. No, the plan can only work if our faith is centered solely *in the Lord Jesus Christ*. Listen to the way Elder Dallin H. Oaks explained this in 1994 to the young women of the Church:

> Faith does not exist by itself. Faith requires an object. It must be faith in something or someone. . . .
>
> If we think we have faith, we should ask, faith in whom or faith in what? For some, faith is nothing more than faith in themselves. That is only self-confidence or self-centeredness. Others have faith in faith, which is something like relying on the power of positive thinking or betting on the proposition that we can get what we want by manipulating the powers within us.

The first principle of the gospel is faith in the Lord Jesus Christ. Without this faith, the prophet Mormon said, we "are not fit to be numbered among the people of his church."[3]

I think most members of the Church would probably say they have faith in Jesus Christ because they know a lot about Him and they believe that He's real. But true faith in the Lord involves much more than that. Here's how President Ezra Taft Benson describes it:

Faith in [Christ] is more that mere acknowledgment that He lives. It is more than professing belief.

Faith in Jesus Christ consists of complete reliance on Him. As God, He has infinite power, intelligence, and love. There is no human problem beyond His capacity to solve. Because He descended below all things, He knows how to help us rise above our daily difficulties.

Faith in Him means believing that even though we do not understand all things, He does. We, therefore, must look to Him "in every thought; doubt not, fear not."[4]

So it isn't enough just to believe in Jesus and to acknowledge that He lives. As President Benson said, true faith in Christ involves "complete reliance on Him," meaning we put our entire life in His capable hands. You may wonder how in the world you develop that kind of deep faith in someone you can't see. The answer is simple. You do it the same way the animated princesses did it—by spending time getting to know your wonderful Prince. Remember, some of those princesses initially had trouble understanding how special their hero truly was. But once they spent more time with their prince and studied his characteristics and attributes, they could finally see his true nature for themselves. As a result, their hearts were softened, and a relationship of love developed that would change each princess's life forever.

President Thomas S. Monson spoke of the importance of taking time to get to know our Prince when he said,

How do we follow him if first we don't find him? And how shall we find him if first we don't seek him? Where and how should we begin this search for Jesus? . . . Before we can successfully undertake a personal search for Jesus, we must first prepare time for him in our lives and room for him in our hearts.[5]

So to truly know Jesus Christ, we must make "time for him in our lives and room for him in our hearts," just like President Monson said. In fact, it's the very thing our Prince has been hoping for. Over and over in the scriptures, He's invited each of us to come closer to Him and to get to know Him. In verse after verse, He's called to us: "Draw near unto me and I will draw near unto you" (D&C 88:63); "Come unto me thy Savior" (D&C 19:41); "Learn of me, and listen to my words" (D&C 19:23); "Look unto me in every thought" (D&C 6:36); "Cleave unto me with all your heart" (D&C 11:19). He invites us to do this because He knows it's the only way we'll learn to have faith in Him—or turn our entire lives over to Him. Just like President Ezra Taft Benson has said, "We must be close to Christ."[6]

You may not know it, but that's one of the most important reasons we're encouraged to study the scriptures. We don't just read them to learn the stories, memorize the scripture mastery verses, or check off a goal in our Personal Progress. We immerse ourselves in those pages so we can get to know our handsome Prince. In the pages of the standard works, we'll learn how He's rescued others and the miracles He's performed in their personal lives. Along with these stories, the scriptures will also give us a thorough description of the Lord's many wonderful characteristics and attributes.

When President Benson searched the Book of Mormon with this purpose in mind, he actually found a long list of characteristics that give us a really good glimpse into the heart of our Prince. Here's the list the prophet read in general conference:

He is Alive (Mosiah 16:9).

He is Constant (2 Nephi 27:23).

He is the Creator (Mosiah 4:9).

He is the Exemplar (2 Nephi 31:9, 10).

He is Generous (2 Nephi 26:24).

He is Godly (2 Nephi 27:23).

He is Good (Moroni 7:12).

He is Gracious (2 Nephi 2:6).
He is the Healer (1 Nephi 11:31).
He is Holy (2 Nephi 9:20).
He is Humble (2 Nephi 31:7).
He is Joyful (3 Nephi 28:10).
He is our Judge (Mosiah 16:10).
He is Just (Mosiah 29:12).
He is Kind (1 Nephi 19:9).
He is the Lawgiver (3 Nephi 15:5).
He is the Liberator (Mosiah 5:8).
He is the Light (Mosiah 16:9).
He is Loving (2 Nephi 26:24).
He is the Mediator (2 Nephi 2:27).
He is Merciful (1 Nephi 8:8).
He is Mighty (1 Nephi 4:1).
He is Miraculous (2 Nephi 27:23).
He is Obedient (2 Nephi 31:7).
He is Omnipotent (Mosiah 4:9).
He is Omniscient (1 Nephi 9:6).
He is our Redeemer (1 Nephi 10:6).
He is the Resurrection (2 Nephi 2:8).
He is Righteous (2 Nephi 1:19).
He is the Ruler (2 Nephi 29:7).
He is our Savior (2 Nephi 25:20).
He is Sinless (Mosiah 15:5).
He is Truthful (Ether 3:12).
He is Wise (Mosiah 4:9).[7]

If you ask me, that's a perfect description of everything a Prince Charming should be.

However, like we already said, in order to develop a personal relationship with Jesus Christ, it's not enough just to know about Him. You can know a lot about someone's life and still not know that person at all. Think about the teen girls who can tell you every detail about their celebrity crush. Yes, they may know where that guy was born and what his favorite food is and what he likes to do in his spare time, but they still don't actually *know* him, right? Well, the same thing applies to your relationship with your

Savior. Remember, even the devil and his angels knew who He was (see Mark 5:2–7; Acts 19:15), but that didn't mean a thing. If we truly want to *know* Jesus Christ like each movie princess knew her prince, our relationship with Him must go much deeper than that.

One way we can get to know our Prince better is by learning to hear His voice for ourselves. In other words, we need to understand how to *communicate with Him* on a daily basis. Of course, one of the most common ways our Prince speaks to us is through the scriptures and the words of the prophets and apostles. Jesus Himself has told us that when we read the standard works or listen to the Brethren, it's just like He's talking to us personally: "What I the Lord have spoken, I have spoken . . . *whether by mine own voice or by the voice of my servants, it is the same* (D&C 1:38; emphasis added; see also D&C 18:33–36).

But there's another way our Savior communicates with us, and it's even more intimate and personal. He does it by speaking directly to us Himself. Now, I'm not talking about hearing an audible voice like when your parents or friends talk to you. Jesus Christ speaks a little differently than that. As Nephi told his older brothers, we have to learn to "*feel* his words" (1 Nephi 17:45; emphasis added). Here's how our Prince explains it: "Yea, behold, *I will tell you in your mind and in your heart*, by the Holy Ghost, which shall come upon you and which shall dwell in your heart" (D&C 8:2; emphasis added). I hope you noticed in that scripture that it's not the Holy Ghost talking to us—it's *the Prince Himself* who will communicate with our heart and mind through the power of the Spirit.

In other words, we experience the voice of our Prince not through our ears but through the thoughts of our mind and the feelings of our heart. Think about how the Lord said He "[spoke] peace to [Oliver Cowdery's] mind" in Doctrine and Covenants 6:23. He also told Oliver, "Thou knowest that thou hast inquired of me and I did enlighten thy mind" (D&C 6:15). That's a pretty amazing way to communicate. Like what happened to Enos in the Book of Mormon, the "voice of the Lord" really can "[come] into

[our] mind" so our Prince can tell us everything He wants us to know and do (Enos 1:10; see also verse 5).

There are many people in the scriptures who learned to hear the Prince's voice for themselves. Nephi heard it (1 Nephi 17:8). Moroni heard it (Ether 12:26–29). The brother of Jared heard it (Ether 2:14). Enoch heard it (Moses 6:32). The people of Alma heard it as well (Mosiah 24:16). And the same privilege can be ours if we'll draw close to our Prince and learn what His voice actually sounds like. I promise that once we do this, our life will never be the same.

As our relationship with our Prince grows stronger, the next things we need to do are "turn to [Him] with full purpose of heart, and put [our] trust in him" (Mosiah 7:33). I believe the key word in that verse is *trust*. That's because we can't just come to *know* the Lord—we must also learn to truly *trust* Him.

The movie *Aladdin* does a beautiful job illustrating the importance of trusting our Prince. Do you remember the scene when Jasmine and Aladdin were talking on the rooftop and the soldiers suddenly burst in the door? Aladdin knew exactly how to escape, but instead of charging ahead, he took a moment to reach out his hand to the princess and ask, "Do you trust me?" He knew she was going to have to take a daring leap in order to be free, and he wanted to make sure she trusted him to lead the way. The question popped up a second time when Aladdin offered to take her on a magic carpet ride. Because Jasmine was hesitant to climb on the carpet, Aladdin again held out his hand and asked, "Do you trust me?" He was trying to help the princess see that she was putting her life in the hands of someone she could trust.

In similar fashion, our Prince is reaching out to us and asking, "Do you trust me?"(see Psalm 37:5; 64:10; 2 Nephi 4:34; 22:2). Our answer is important because He's going to ask us to do some difficult things in order to make it out of the lair. In the scenes ahead, we're going to have to walk some unfamiliar paths, leave behind stuff we love, and go through some experiences we may not be comfortable with. Like Jasmine, the only way we can succeed is by developing such deep and abiding trust in Christ that we're willing to do anything He asks—even if it isn't easy, even if it doesn't make sense, and even if others around us don't approve or understand. Jesus Christ really can save us from the awful monster, but we must trust Him enough to place our lives in His all-powerful hands.

If, as you've been reading this chapter, you've realized that you don't yet have the kind of relationship with Jesus Christ I've been describing, then it's time for you to do something about that. Like the movie princesses did with their princes, it's time for you to "seek this Jesus" with all your might, mind, and strength (Ether 12:41). Remember, your Prince has promised you, "Ye shall seek me, and find me, when ye shall search for me with all your heart" (Jeremiah 29:13). You'll find Him by spending time in the scriptures, pondering, and praying until Christ finally becomes much more than the man wearing a red robe in a picture—He becomes *real* to you. Soon your heart will soften and you'll be ready to truly trust Him and put your life in His capable hands. More than anything, He's waiting to ransom you from the villain and change you back into a pure and beautiful princess.

If you're ready, it's time to press on to the next scene of our story. I think you'll find that, in this scene, our Hero has some important things He wants to say.

For Additional Study

I saved some of my favorite quotes for this particular section. Read through each one and take some time to journal how you feel about Jesus Christ and how you hope to deepen and improve your personal relationship with Him.

Elder F. Enzio Busche:

> What is [the] real treasure that will enable us to stand in happiness and joy, in confidence, and with power each day of our lives? It [is] . . . to develop a close relationship with Christ, the Savior, the Redeemer, the Messiah, Jehovah, the Only Begotten of Elohim, and let him and his Spirit take possession of our lives. . . . I am speaking about the treasure of having found Christ, of being able to know him—not merely to know all about him, but really to know him.[8]

President Henry B. Eyring:

We promise to take His name upon us. That means we must see ourselves as His. We will put Him first in our lives. We will want what He wants rather than what we want or what the world teaches us to want.[9]

Brigham Young:

The greatest and most important of all requirements of our Father in heaven and of his Son Jesus Christ, is . . . to believe in Jesus Christ, confess him, seek to him, cling to him, make friends with him. Take a course to open and to keep open communication with your Elder Brother or file-leader—our Savior.[10]

A DANGEROUS DISTRACTION

TELL ME, WHEN you think about the Lord speaking to you, what do you imagine Him saying? Do you hear Him telling you how much He loves you or how wonderful He thinks you are? Do you envision Him offering positive words of admiration, comfort, and reassurance? I know that's what most of us would want to hear from our handsome prince. However, you must remember that you're trapped in the clutches of a dangerous villain, and your Hero can think of nothing else but setting you free. So His most important instructions probably won't sound soft, mushy, loving, or sentimental. Instead, it will actually sound more like this:

> I am Alpha and Omega, Christ the Lord; yea, even I am he, the beginning and the end, the Redeemer of the world. . . . Therefore I command you to repent. . . . For behold, I, God, have suffered these things for all, that they might not suffer if they would repent. . . . Wherefore I command you again to repent. (D&C 19:1, 15–16, 20)

Why such harsh words from your Prince Charming? Why would He speak to you that way? It's because He's intent on telling you the truth. Jesus Christ understands what's happened to you since you left your Father's celestial mansion, so there's no way He's going to sit in the enemy's cave with you and sing you love songs. No, He knows the only way you can become a princess again is if you repent. Remember, in the fourth article of faith, repentance is the second step in His strategy or gospel plan. So rather than lulling you with soft, sweet words, He's more likely to grab your face in His hands and make sure you're paying attention, and then He'll say it over and over until He's sure you're really listening: your faith *must* be accompanied by repentance in order for Him to free you from the monster and get you out of the lair.

In the scriptures, the Prince's servants remind us again and again that the Lord can only save us if we choose to repent. Here are just a few examples: "And now, ought ye not to tremble and repent of your sins, and remember that only in and through Christ ye can be saved?" (Mosiah 16:13); "Therefore, blessed are they who will repent and hearken unto the voice of the Lord their God; for these are they that shall be saved" (Helaman 12:23); "Repent all ye ends of the earth, and . . . have faith in [Christ], that ye may be saved" (Moroni 7:34).

However, I know some young women who believe repentance doesn't really apply to them—that it's mostly for people who've done something really wicked or wrong. If that describes you, I want you to stop and think for a minute about your dragon nature. Think about all the times you've acted like a selfish little monster rather than a royal princess. Think about the things you've done that you hope no one ever finds out about. Maybe then you'll see why repentance doesn't just apply to murderers and drug dealers, but to every single one of us. Elder Russell M. Nelson captures it this way:

> While the Lord insists on our repentance, most people don't feel such a compelling need. They include themselves among those who try to be good. They have no evil intent. Yet the Lord is clear in His message that *all* need to repent.[1]

Now, I'm sure that you've heard Young Women or Sunday School lessons where repentance is explained like this: First, you recognize you've done something wrong. Then you confess your sin and ask for forgiveness. And then you promise you'll never do that thing again. Sound familiar? The problem is, at some point most of us end up committing that same sin we promised we'd stop. So we repent again, and then we sin again, and we repent again, and then we sin again. The cycle continues over and over. Like Eustace, our dragon skin just keeps coming back, no matter how many times we try to scratch it off.

I'd like to suggest that we go through this cycle because we haven't yet learned what it means to repent. President Dieter F. Uchtdorf said repentance isn't just a change of behavior—it's "a change of mind and heart."[2] In other words, repentance isn't so much about stopping certain outward behaviors, but about experiencing a lasting change in the thought patterns of our mind and the feelings of our heart. To make it a little easier to understand, consider some synonyms for the word *change*. They include *modify*, *adjust*, *reconstruct*, *reverse*, *switch*, and *remodel*.[3] So to repent, our mind and heart must be completely reconstructed, remodeled, and modified. Our dragon thoughts and feelings must be switched with the thoughts and feelings of a royal princess.

It's a lot like weeding a garden. To get the weeds out, you can't just pop off the tops. You have to dig down under the soil and pull out the root of the weed. It's the only way to be sure they'll never grow back. The same thing goes with our dragon nature. If all we do is try to modify our outward behavior, we're only popping off the top of the weeds and our sins will come back again and again. So to truly repent, we need to let our Prince help us dig the nasty dragon roots out of our hearts and minds. Once those stubborn roots are gone, we'll not only think like royal princesses once again but also have what the Apostle Paul calls the "mind of Christ" (1 Corinthians 2:16).

So what are these dragon roots that live deep in our hearts? You might be surprised at my answer. They're *lies*—our enemy's horrible, conniving, deceitful *lies*. Just like roots that live underground, these lies are really good at hiding—so good, in fact, that most of the time we don't even know they're there. We go about our lives thinking everything is fine, but underneath the surface, Satan's lies continue to grow and thrive deep in the corners of our hearts. I bet you've got some lies living inside you that you don't even know about. If you don't believe me, consider Rapunzel's story. Although she was a sweet, happy girl on the outside, under-neath the surface, there were some dangerous lies that had taken root in the princess's heart and mind—and she didn't even realize it.

Think for a minute about the song Rapunzel sings in the beginning of *Tangled*. She charms us by singing about all the fun stuff she does while living in the tower. She talks about how she reads books, paints, and plays the guitar. She tackles puzzles, darts, and papier-mâché. She sews, sketches, and makes home-made candles. At first glance, Rapunzel's life seems pretty great. She has Pascal to play with and a lot of fun and interesting things to do. But even though things look all sweet and happy, the truth is that Rapunzel's entire existence is based on some big, fat lies. She believes that Gothel is her mother and the outside world is an awful, horrible place. So she stays in her tower and entertains herself when she could be back in her parents' kingdom enjoying a life of happiness, love, and family affection.

Believe it or not, the exact same thing has happened to you. The villain and his sneaky servants have lied to you just like Gothel lied to Rapunzel. You've probably heard the scriptures describe Satan as "the father of all lies," who seeks "to deceive and to blind men" (Moses 4:4), but you may never have realized that verse was talking to *you*. To make matters worse, the villain and his side-kicks have been so good at lying to you that you probably haven't even realized they've done it. All this time you've been living your life and doing all kinds of fun activities, just like Rapunzel. But deep in your heart, the enemy's lies have grown bigger, stronger, and more poisonous by the day.

How in the world could such a thing have happened? It's simple, really. First, your enemy watched your life carefully. Patiently, he waited until just the right moment, and then he sent in his servants to do his dirty work. Ariel suffered this fate in the early scenes of *The Little Mermaid*. I don't know if you noticed, but Flotsam and Jetsam didn't approach the princess when she was playing happily with Flounder or talking to Sebastian. No, the sneaky eels waited until something terrible happened—King Triton destroyed his daughter's precious collection. At the moment

Ariel was at her weakest and most vulnerable, Ursula's two evil assistants slipped in and began to whisper in her ear that they knew the perfect solution to her problem. Using subtle language, they eventually convinced Ariel to visit the sea witch's cavern. They assured her that Ursula knew exactly how to make all the little mermaid's dreams come true.

Again, Satan and his sidekicks work the same way in your life. Just like Flotsam and Jetsam, they wait for just the right moment—a moment when you are weak and vulnerable, just like Ariel. Then they sneak in and tell you lies designed especially for you. And they lie to you so subtly and quietly, you probably think the ideas are coming from your own head. Just like Ariel, you have no idea you are being conned by the greatest con artists of all time.

Now I know, at this point, you may be thinking, *Hold on. I haven't believed any of Satan's lies. I've actually watched myself choose the right in many different situations. So this can't be part of my princess story.* If so, let me remind you that Satan is a master at not only lying to us but also *blinding us* to his lies. To show you what I mean, let's go right back to Ursula in her cavern. We already talked about how Flotsam and Jetsam convinced Ariel to go see her, but now we need to listen closely to the plan Ursula proposes.

In Ursula's clever little song, she tells the mermaid all she's trying to do is help poor souls find a little happiness. Into her cavern they swim, looking for answers to their problems, and Ursula shows them a solution that appears to make all their dreams come true. It isn't until later that they find out her spell isn't magic at all—it's just a trick that leaves them trapped in her evil clutches. Can you see how she *blinded* the merpeople to her terrible lies? If you're wondering how Satan has told you similar lies (and blinded you to those lies), let me ask you one simple question. Have you ever been sad or depressed like Ariel was and heard a quiet little voice in your head say, "If only I could have *that*, then I would be happy"? Maybe *that* was a new cell phone, better clothes, or a spot on the cheerleading squad. Maybe *that* was more likes on social media, more music, or tickets to see that band you love so much. Did you ever stop and ask where that little voice was coming from? Well, now you know it's Satan's sidekicks trying to convince you that worldly things will solve all your problems and bring you the happiness you're so desperately searching for. Of all the lies our enemy tells, I think this one is probably one of the most common and also the most successful.

The problem with this particular lie is that it *does* feel good to crank up your speakers or spend a few hours online. It *does* feel good to watch movies all night long and binge on all the ice cream in your freezer. These things definitely make you forget all about your spiritual death for a little while. But these activities can never solve your problem in the long run. Instead, they only provide a temporary fix, and that fix is so enticing that it keeps you coming back for more. Suddenly, *all* you can think about is being on social media, shopping, or reading that brand-new novel. And that's exactly how the sneaky villain gets you. He knows that once you believe worldly things will bring you happiness, you'll continue to turn to those things again and again, and you'll forget about the Prince and life outside the dragon's lair.

One day as I was researching the concept of the princess and the dragon, I came across a little cartoon that perfectly illustrates what I'm talking about. Take a look and see what you think. (I love how it includes a two-headed monster!)

"The Knight, the Princess and the Dragon" by Monika Suska; used with permission.

Consider what's happened to the princess in this picture. She's so caught up in playing the dragon's games that she hasn't even noticed the prince standing there waiting to rescue her. In fact, the princess doesn't even look like she wants to be rescued. Instead, she's caught up in the intoxicating pleasure of her entertaining toys. Is there any chance the same thing has happened to you?

In this scene of the story, the time has come to answer what may be a difficult question: Do you spend more time thinking about the Prince or about the things in the dragon world? One way you can know is to look at what you turn to when you're feeling stressed, tired, upset, or even bored. Do you turn on the TV, text your friends, or sit down in front of your computer? Do you watch a chick flick, eat ice cream, or escape into a good book? Do you hardly give the Prince a second thought? If so, this cartoon is showing you a picture of *your* life. In short, the villain has succeeded in distracting you with the trivial things of the dragon world. He's lied to you and made you believe these things will make you feel better and soothe the yearnings of your restless heart.

The worst part about this particular lie is that Satan isn't just telling it to distract you—he's telling it to introduce you to a dangerous sin. It's the sin of *idolatry*. If you're wondering what idolatry has to do with watching TV or spending time on the Internet, listen to Christian author Timothy Keller's definition of an idol. I think it may cause you to see your favorite things in a whole new light.

> What is an idol? It is anything more important to you than God, anything that absorbs your heart and imagination more than God, anything you seek to give you what only God can give.
>
> A counterfeit god is anything so central and essential to your life that, should you lose it, your life would feel hardly worth living. An idol has such a controlling position in your heart that you can spend most of your passion and energy, your emotional and financial resources, on it without a second thought. . . . An idol is whatever you look at and say, in your heart of hearts, "If I have that, then I'll feel my life has meaning, then I'll know I have value, then I'll feel significant and secure."[4]

That hits pretty close to home, don't you think? None of us likes to see ourselves as idolaters, but if we're turning to worldly things to find happiness instead of our Prince, then those things really have become counterfeit gods to us.

Now, please don't think I'm saying that it's a sin to listen to music or to sit down and watch TV. I have a smart phone stocked with music, I watch TV with my family, and I also participate in social media. The problem comes when we start to use these things to renew us, recharge us, and make us forget about life in the dragon world. Worldly things become idols when we turn to *them* to be saved rather than the One who really does have the power to rescue us. Remember, only our Prince can "[satisfy] the longing soul, and [fill] the hungry soul with goodness" (Psalm 107:9). If we're trying to fill our souls with something else, we'll never make it out of the dragon's lair.

We're going to talk later about how to repent of our idolatry and turn "with full purpose of heart" to our Prince (Jacob 6:5). But we can't do that yet because we're still not finished with this scene in our princess story. You see, while we now know that our enemy has lied to us and distracted us with fun and entertaining things in the dragon world, we also need to realize that he's lied to us about a bunch of *other* things too. So let's dive a little deeper into enemy territory and see if we can uncover a few more of the villain's devious, underhanded lies. By helping us uncover these sneaky falsehoods, our Prince is beginning to show us how to break free from the clutches of the enemy.

For Additional Study

One of my favorite quotes on repentance is from President Ezra Taft Benson. He said,

> Repentance means more than simply a reformation of behavior. Many men and women in the world demonstrate great willpower and self-discipline in overcoming bad habits and the weaknesses of the flesh. Yet at the same time they give no thought to the Master, sometimes even openly rejecting Him. Such changes of behavior, even if in a positive direction, do not constitute true repentance.

> Faith in the Lord Jesus Christ is the foundation upon which sincere and meaningful repentance must be built. If we truly seek to put away sin, we must first look to Him who is the Author of our salvation.[5]

Now turn to the Bible Dictionary and look up the heading "Repentance." Journal what you learn about the Greek word for *repent* and also about the topic of repentance. Are you beginning to see this subject any differently as a result of our princess story? Why or why not?

Two really amazing articles you can read about the enemy and his lies are "Be Not Deceived" by Dallin H. Oaks in the November 2004 *Ensign* and "Truth and Lies" by Jennifer Nuckols in the October 2009 *Ensign*. I think it would be great if after reading Sister Nuckols's article you did the same thing she did and tried to outline the lies you've accepted in your own personal life. (We're going to talk about this a lot more in the next scene of our story.)

A LOAD OF LIES

WHEN I WAS in high school, I lived in a city that had few LDS kids. Because I spent so much time around peers who didn't share my standards, I faced typical teenage temptations with the Word of Wisdom, inappropriate media, and with dating. But I thought that's all I really needed to worry about when it came to Satan. I had no idea the villain's plans for me were both cunning and complex, and involved much more than just my giving in to those types of worldly temptations. During those sensitive teen years, Satan used his lies for sinister purposes that would affect me well into my adulthood.

What did the villain do that was so sinister? Well, in addition to tempting me with worldly things, he also did everything he could to wound me, incapacitate me, and destroy me. We'll talk about several ways he does so in this scene of the story, but one way my enemy wounded me was by taking the bad things that happened to me and using them as fuel for some extremely vicious lies. I believe the same thing happens to each of us. To show you what I mean, let's start with what goes on in the lives of our individual families.

I know we hear a lot in the Church about the importance of families and that our family can be together forever if we're sealed in the temple. But let's talk for a minute about what happens in our families while we're living here on earth. I think by now we all understand that we're spiritually dead because of the Fall, but what we often forget is that our family members are also spiritually dead, which means our parents and siblings have turned into dragons just like us.[1] When you put all those dragons together under one roof, things can get pretty ugly as we try to live together and deal with each other on a daily basis.

I'm guessing that at one time or another, a member of your family has roasted you with dragon breath by saying mean and hurtful things, things that cut you to the core. Even though we know we're not supposed to treat each other that way, brothers and sisters still do it all the time—and unfortunately, so do parents. Because family members feel so comfortable at home, they tend to let their dragon nature come out in all its ugliness. As a result, parents and siblings often end up wounding each other rather than treating each other with the love, patience, and respect family members deserve.

Of course, our family problems can get a lot worse than just saying mean and insulting remarks to one another. Dragons can do a lot of terrible things to each other while living inside the lair—so terrible, in fact, that some families even break up altogether. The abuse suffered at the hands of a family member can be extremely devastating, especially when it happens at a young and tender age. And I'm not just talking about physical or sexual abuse; I also mean emotional abuse (like a parent being unnecessarily controlling or emotionally manipulative). The pain inflicted on us by our family members can be one of the most difficult parts of living as prisoners in the enemy's lair.

This is the point where Satan shows how mean and despicable he really is. Any decent person would have compassion for the difficult things we go through in families, but the villain isn't decent by any stretch of the imagination—and he isn't compassionate either. Rather than taking it easy on us in the sensitive areas of our lives, he instead takes the very things that hurt us most and uses those to drive his lies deeper into our hearts and minds.

For example, let's say your father left your family when you were young. You may think that didn't affect you much while you were growing up, but I bet Satan and his sidekicks used it as an opportunity to whisper, "It's all your fault. Your father left because of something *you* did." Or perhaps their lies sounded more like this: "Everyone will abandon you. You'll never have anyone to trust or rely on." You may not even realize these kinds of lies live deep inside you, but if you look closely enough, I'm sure you'll find some damaging falsehoods hiding quietly in the corners of your heart and mind.

It could be that an ill loved one died even though you'd prayed and prayed that person would get better, so your enemy jumped at the chance to whisper, "Heavenly Father doesn't answer your prayers." Or maybe you have a family member who is extremely hard to please, so the adversary joined the criticism with a chorus of, "You're worthless. You can never do anything right." It could be you have a parent who has a hard time communicating love to you, so the villain's sidekicks suggested, "It's because you're unlovable. How could anyone love someone as useless and annoying as you?" The worst part is, the minute these lies worm their way inside our heads, they actually become part of us—part of our personality and part of the way we relate to the outside world. And we don't even realize it happened.

Even if you come from a healthy family that treats each other with love and respect, that doesn't mean Satan hasn't tried to wound you or lie to you. Difficult things also happen to us outside of our family, like with friends, guys, teachers, leaders, and even life in general. These stressful trials can leave us feeling hurt, betrayed, rejected, unloved, and alone. Take all that suffering, add to it all the shame and guilt we feel over our sins, and we end up with a deep void inside that we have no idea how to fill. Most of the time we don't call it a void—we just know we feel depressed. Or worthless. Or invisible. Or unimportant. Like we'll never, ever be enough. Because we want so much to be accepted, loved, and valued, we begin searching for someone or something to fill our void—someone to tell us it will be okay, to tell us *we're* okay. We just want to know that we *matter* in this discouraging and complicated world.

Now, here's where Satan really shines as a liar and deceiver. He knows all about the emptiness we feel while living in the lair, and he uses his lies to get us to fill our void in any other way than turning to our Prince. In the last chapter, we talked about how he talks us into filling our void with worldly things, but remember that Satan's falsehoods take many different forms. In fact, most of the time his lies are disguised as helpful answers to some of life's most difficult questions.

For instance, one sneaky lie the villain used on me sounded like this: "You can find happiness and worth by gaining the approval of others." I'm sad to say that this falsehood worked really well on me. I thought being popular would somehow prove I was valuable—fill my void. So throughout my teenage years, I said and did only those things that would make other people like me. When I interacted with others, I hid my real self behind a mask and tried to do all I could to fit in. I never realized I'd been lied to by the enemy. But in truth, underneath the weed of my outward behavior was a terrible dragon root. I'd been deceived into thinking the only way to be happy was to gain the favor and acceptance of others.

The trouble with living to be popular is that it places our feet on really shaky ground. If others like us, we're happy, but if they don't, we're not. We're up one day and down the next. To make matters worse, we're never able to be our true selves. We always have to try to impress people, and we end up doing things we don't want to do just so others will think we're cool. It's an unstable way to live, which is exactly why Satan tries to talk us into doing it. Sadly, I spent many years chasing the approval of others before I finally realized I'd been deceived by a cruel and deceitful enemy.

Another common lie our enemy tells us goes like this: "You will feel valuable if you are the best at everything you do." With this subtle falsehood, Satan tries to convince us that if we work hard enough, we can prove our worth through our performance. So we kill ourselves trying to get perfect grades or be a perfect singer, dancer, debater, musician, or athlete. If we believe this persuasive lie, perfectionism becomes our identity and we do all we can to hide our weaknesses and only show the world our impressive strengths. Our enemy deceives us into thinking that perfect performance will prove we're important in the eyes of the world, our family, and even our Father in Heaven.

The problem with this lie is that every single one of us falls short at times, so if we base our worth on our performance, Satan will always have a way to shame us when we fail to live up to that standard. He'll gleefully mock us for that C grade, the bad day at soccer practice, or the time we forgot our homework. "See?" he'll whisper. "You'll never measure up. You'll never be enough. You'll never amount to anything, no matter how hard you try." Sometimes the audacity of the villain really blows my mind. First he deceives us into serving the god of perfectionism, and then he ridicules us every time we mess up. It's a vicious cycle that keeps us stuck like a mouse on a wheel—continually trying to be perfect but never really able to get there.

Another successful lie that works on women both young and old sounds like this: "Your life will be amazing if you can just make yourself more thin and beautiful." I started believing this lie as a teenager, and it continued to haunt me into my twenties and thirties. I believed if I could just fit into a smaller size, all my problems would finally be solved. But when I compared my body to the size-0 models in the magazines, the villain's awful sneers flooded my mind again and again: "You're fat. You're ugly. You need to lose weight." Sadly, I never realized those thoughts were coming from an enemy who hated me and was trying to make me miserable. Instead, I thought it was my own voice—and I believed it was telling me the truth.

There's another deceptive lie Satan and his sidekicks use specifically on women and girls. See if it sounds familiar: "You'll find your ultimate happiness and fulfillment through the world of romance." Today's world abounds with chick flicks and romance novels that try hard to convince us of this. Over and over, we're told that all we need in life is to find an amazing guy who will love us unconditionally. Finally, we'd have someone who "completes" us, someone who is captivated by our little quirks and eccentricities, someone who treasures us for who we really are. It's just another version of the princess story that seems to have its own happily ever after.

But something dangerous happens when we choose to believe this particular lie. The opposite sex becomes a false god to us.

Slowly and subtly, we rely on the attention of boys to determine our worth and value. Satan especially loves telling this lie to those of us who don't have a close relationship with our father. Without even realizing it, we may become boy crazy as a way of getting the male attention we haven't been getting at home. But even if we're close to our dads, it's still easy to get caught up in the sparkling allure of the world of romance and affection.

There's certainly nothing wrong with the romantic relationship between a man and a woman, but if we allow romance to become our god, we'll find that it can never fill our inner void the way we think it will. That's because as wonderful as guys are, they're struggling with a dragon nature just like we are. And a dragon can't save another dragon from the misery of the lair. I know the attention of a cute boy fills you with bubbly excitement for a little while, but doesn't that bubbly feeling always burn itself out eventually? It just goes to show that the world of romance can never change our dragon hearts or free us from life in the lair. There's only one prince with the ability to save us and deliver us. Jesus Christ really is our only knight in shining armor.

Another lie that gets a lot of attention in today's modern world goes like this: "You can overcome all the problems in your life by building up your self-esteem." An insightful article in the January 2014 *New Era* points out the danger of this particular lie:

> When people encourage you to focus on building self-esteem (rather than recognizing eternal self-worth), you may be tempted to think you'll be happier with yourself if you focus on building you. That's the tricky thing about this lie. It seems so logical that self-esteem should be all about you, but that's how the adversary tricks you. If he can get you so obsessed with "improving" yourself (typically with the outward things the world values) that you're totally focused on *you*, then it will distract you from all the people around you whom you could be helping.[2]

See how sneaky the adversary's lies can be? In the moment, they seem to make a lot of sense, but in the end, they just keep us focused on the wrong things and looking to the wrong source for salvation.

Of all the lies the villain tells us, I think the worst ones are the lies about our Prince. More than anything, Satan wants to make us doubt that Christ loves us and has the ability to save us. It's the same strategy Gothel used on Rapunzel. In the forest when Rapunzel first hinted she thought Eugene liked her, Gothel immediately shot back, "Rapunzel, that's demented! Why would he like you? Look at you. Don't be a dummy." Then later on the beach when the two brothers knocked Eugene unconscious and tied him to the wheel of a ship, Gothel used the scenario to convince Rapunzel that her prince had forsaken her, that he'd left her in favor of the crown. Unfortunately, the princess chose to believe this lie and ran straight into the arms of her enemy. So anytime your mind starts to question the power and love of your Prince, you can know without a doubt that you've been lied to. If you believe the lies the villain is telling you, it won't just prevent you from being rescued—it will break your Prince's tender heart. Elder Jeffrey R. Holland explains it like this:

> Consider, for example, the Savior's benediction. . . . "Peace I leave with you, my peace I give unto you. . . . Let not your heart be troubled, neither let it be afraid." . . .
>
> That may be one of the Savior's commandments that is, even in the hearts of otherwise faithful Latter-day Saints, almost universally disobeyed; and yet I wonder whether our resistance to this invitation could be any more grievous to the Lord's merciful heart. . . .
>
> In that same spirit, I am convinced that none of us can appreciate how deeply it wounds the loving heart of the Savior of the world when he finds that his people do not feel confident in his care or secure in his hands or trust in his commandments.[3]

You may be wondering how these kinds of lies—lies about ourselves, our relationships, our lives, and even our Prince—take root in our hearts and minds. I mean, you'd think we'd never fall for anything coming out of the mouth of the evil villain. But the truth is that it's easy for his lies to masquerade as truth. It happens through such a subtle process that we often don't realize it until it's too late.

We fall for Satan's lies when we begin to listen to what Satan's sidekicks are quietly saying. Unfortunately, their lies are so subtle and sneaky that we tend to think the ideas are coming from our own head. Slowly (and often subconsciously) we begin to dwell on their lies and think about them throughout the day. Eventually we become comfortable with these thoughts, and we reach the point where we *agree* with the enemy's lies, deciding in our mind that he's telling the truth. At that point, Satan no longer has to whisper his lies to us because we start telling them to ourselves. With that, his lies begin to take over our thoughts, our feelings, and our lives.

For a perfect example of this progression, let's go back to the way Gothel convinced Rapunzel that Eugene was only interested in the crown. If you remember, when Gothel first tried to tell her Eugene was no good, Rapunzel fought hard against that lie, adamantly declaring it wasn't true. But over time, Gothel produced an elaborate scheme that preyed on Rapunzel's deepest fears and insecurities. Slowly, her lies infiltrated the princess's heart and mind. Once Rapunzel saw Eugene sailing away in his ship, she ran into Gothel's arms and said, "You were right." The consequences of her choice to believe were devastating. Rapunzel had actually been set free by her prince, but because she heeded her enemy's lies, *she willingly returned to her life as a captive.*

As hard as it may be to hear, the same thing holds true for each of us. When we believe Satan's horrible lies, it gives our enemy power to keep us in bondage. What's worse, it allows his sneaky servants to enter our hearts and take control of our thoughts and feelings. In other words, they really can start to *possess* us. Stay with me—we don't talk much today about being possessed by evil spirits. That seems to belong to the world of horror movies rather than our everyday lives. But we've got to remember that it happened all the time both in the Bible and the Book of Mormon. When we read these stories, we tend to picture possessed people as ones who foam at the mouth, gnash their teeth, or do something even crazier. But I'm here to tell you that we can be influenced by an evil spirit and not even know it. I'll prove my point by telling a little story found in the book of Luke.

This particular account takes place well into Jesus's earthly ministry. After returning from the Mount of Transfiguration with Peter, James, and John, the Lord began preparing to go to Jerusalem. He sent messengers to a Samaritan village to see if He could stop there on the way, but the village wasn't willing to receive Him. Infuriated, James and John defended their Master by asking Jesus, "Lord, wilt thou that we command fire to come down from heaven, and consume them, even as Elias did?" But the Lord turned to His two Apostles, rebuked them, and said, "*Ye know not what manner of spirit ye are of*" (Luke 9:54–55; emphasis added).

Hmm. "What manner of *spirit* ye are of." Want to guess what the footnote says on the word *spirit*? It says "Spirits, Evil or Unclean." In other words, the Lord was telling James and John that an evil spirit was influencing them and they didn't even know it. It's a pretty shocking revelation, don't you think? If such a thing could happen to two of the Lord's own apostles, then it could definitely happen to each of us. In 1995, Elder Boyd K. Packer warned modern-day youth of this reality:

> Now, young people, pay attention! . . . I must tell you so that you cannot possibly misunderstand. "There are many spirits which are false spirits." There can be counterfeit revelations, promptings from the devil, temptations! As long as you live, in one way or another the adversary will try to lead you astray. . . .
>
> The Prophet Joseph Smith said that "*nothing is a greater injury to the children of men than to be under the influence of a false spirit when they think they have the Spirit of God.*"[4]

For another example of the power the devil's angels have to possess us, let's turn to Korihor's story in the Book of Mormon. You probably know that Korihor was a wicked man who spent his days telling the Nephites that "there should be no Christ" (Alma 30:12) and that those who believed in such things were victims of a "frenzied mind" (Alma 30:16). But the story really gets interesting when Alma confronts the man with these words:

> Behold, I know that thou believest, *but thou art possessed with a lying spirit*, and ye have put off the Spirit of God that it may have

no place in you; but the devil has power over you, and he doth carry you about, working devices that he may destroy the children of God. (Alma 30:42; emphasis added)

Please note that Korihor was "possessed with a lying spirit," but he wasn't writhing on the floor, cutting himself, or falling in the fire like we see in the New Testament (see Mark 5:5; Matthew 17:15). Instead, he was a powerful public speaker who'd attracted an enormous following. If you ask me, this story breaks the stereotype of what it looks like to be possessed by one of Satan's sidekicks. More important, it should open our eyes to the possibility that an evil spirit could also be dwelling inside of *us*.

If you're thinking there's no way that could ever happen to you, let me ask you a few simple questions. Have you ever experienced a "spirit of heaviness" (Isaiah 61:3) where you felt depressed and numb and quit caring about the important things in life? How about a "spirit of jealousy" (Numbers 5:14), a "spirit of contention" (3 Nephi 11:29), or a "spirit of fear" (2 Timothy 1:7)? Perhaps you've been filled with a "spirit of the world" (1 Corinthians 2:12) where you obsessed over a certain TV show, rock star, or Internet site. Or maybe you were overtaken by a "spirit of bondage" (Romans 8:15) where you struggled with an addiction that you just couldn't seem to break. Now you know where those spirits were coming from. Just like James and John, we too can be possessed by Satan's sidekicks. They're so sneaky that they can enter our mind and take control of our thoughts and actions without us even realizing it.

I believe that's exactly what happened to Mary Magdalene, the first woman to witness Christ's Resurrection. Did you know that, long before that incredible moment, Jesus cast "seven devils" out of her (Luke 8:2)? In earlier years, I pictured those seven devils causing Mary to tear her hair out, go into convulsions, or scream at everyone who passed by. But now I see that she may have been possessed by something simple like a spirit of envy, a spirit of lust, or a spirit of greed. It just goes to show that when Satan's servants gain access to our minds and hearts, it doesn't always look like something out of a horror movie. Instead, it can happen so slowly and quietly that we hardly even notice it's happened.

I hope you're beginning to see the many ways each of us has been influenced by the enemy and his angels. Led by their cunning whispers, we've turned to entertainment, food, or social media to fill our void. We try to make ourselves skinnier, get a boyfriend, or have perfect grades. We focus on becoming more popular or building up our self-esteem. Though none of those things filled our void in the long run, somehow we are convinced it was the only way to find a little happiness in the moment.

Now our Prince is standing before us, and He wants to deliver us from the "gall of bitterness and . . . the bonds of iniquity" (Moroni 8:14). He knows the pain and anguish we've experienced. He knows all about our inner void. He knows others have wounded us, and He knows the lies we've been talked into believing. He also knows exactly what we need to do to be free from the adversary. If you'll join me in the next scene of our story, the Prince will continue to teach us how to cast off the lies, shed our dragon skin, and become the pure and beautiful princess we were always destined to become.

For Additional Study

Turn to Doctrine and Covenants 46:7. What does this verse teach us about evil spirits and how they work in our individual lives? How do you think you can know when Satan's sidekicks are trying to seduce you? (Try using the footnotes to help you answer that question.)

In your journal, see if you can identify all of the strategies you think the enemy has used on you. In what ways has he tried to introduce you to his sneaky little lies? (If you're like me, it will be a really long list.) Make sure to get really specific and look for the some of the less obvious tactics he and his servants may be using against you in your everyday life. Pray for help to see any of the villain's strategies you've been blind to.

In 2 Nephi 28:22, it says one of our enemy's favorite schemes is using flattery. Take a minute to look up the words *flatter* and *flattery* so you'll have a better idea of what this verse is talking about. Read the following quote from President James E. Faust:

Satan is the world's master in the use of flattery, and he knows the great power of speech, a power his servants often employ. . . . No one would listen to Satan's voice if it sounded harsh or mean. If the devil's voice were unpleasant, it would not persuade people to listen to it.[5]

Can you think of any ways the evil villain has tried to flatter you? Why do you think he uses that particular approach? Did it work on you at the time? Record your answers in your journal, along with any other impressions that come to your mind and heart.

A BROKEN HEART

Take a good look around the dragon's lair, because it 's not going to be your home for much longer. As you study the dingy walls and cold stone floor, think about how difficult it's been to live in this "dark and dreary waste" (1 Nephi 8:7). I know at times life in the lair hasn't seemed that bad. You've had other dragons to play with and lots of fun and interesting things to do. But for just a minute, think about all the dark days—days when a sense of hopelessness or worthlessness flooded your heart; days when you felt lost, alone, or afraid; days when your dragon nature took over and you acted like a selfish little monster. Wouldn't it feel wonderful to shake off the "bands of death, and the chains of hell" once and for all (Alma 5:7)? Wouldn't it feel wonderful to say good-bye to this "[dark] abyss" and step out into the "marvelous light of God" (Mosiah 27:29)?

If so, then these words will be music to your ears: "Arise, shine; for thy light is come, and the glory of the Lord is risen upon thee" (Isaiah 60:1). If you're willing, your Prince is ready to teach you how to leave that dreary cave behind and experience for yourself the "glorious majesty of his kingdom" (Psalm 145:12). I'm not talking about some warm, fuzzy moment that you'll feel occasionally while living the rest of your life as a prisoner. I'm talking about a whole new world of freedom and love that lies just beyond the walls of the dragon's lair.

The scriptures are packed with descriptions of what it feels like to join your Prince in His wonderful kingdom of light. For starters, Alma said there was "nothing so exquisite and sweet" as the joy he felt when he left the lair and joined the Lord in his beautiful and captivating new world (Alma 36:21). Certain Nephites said "no one [could] conceive of the joy which filled [their] souls" (3 Nephi 17:17) when they entered this incredible kingdom of goodness and love. But of all the accounts in the scriptures, I think the story of Lamoni is my favorite. When the "power of God" fell on the young king, "the dark veil of unbelief was . . . cast away from his mind," and the "light of the glory of God . . . infused such joy into his soul" that it "[overcame] his natural frame, and he was carried away in God" (Alma 19:6). Leaving the lair and entering our Prince's kingdom really is the perfect happy ending for our personal princess story.

This shining new world may sound so incredible that you want to run out of the dragon's lair as fast as you possibly can. But before you get too excited, let me remind you that breaking free from your enemy isn't going to be as easy as you might think. Cinderella learned this lesson when she tried to leave her life as a servant and step into the fancy world of the prince's ball. She attempted to enter that world by donning a princess dress created by her little animal friends. But what happened the minute she put on the homemade gown? The wicked stepsisters ripped her dress—and all her precious dreams—to shreds.

Cinderella's experience just goes to show that you'll never get out of the lair by relying on your own plans, your own willpower, or your own ambition. The villain and his servants will beat you back every time. So that means it's time to stop replaying that old scene where you try to scratch off your dragon skin and dress yourself up as a more righteous person. Thankfully, there's a much easier way. Just like Cinderella had her fairy godmother, you have a Prince with magical powers all his own. But unlike the fairy godmother's magic, Christ's supernatural power actually has a name. It's *grace*—His empowering, magnificent, miraculous, amazing *grace*.

If you aren't that familiar with the concept of grace, let me take a minute to fill you in. The Bible Dictionary says grace is a "divine means of help or strength, given through the bounteous mercy and love of Jesus Christ."[1] However, in order to break free from the lair, we need to know a lot more about our Prince's grace than that. Yes, Christ's grace is His power to help us—but we need to know how we actually receive that help and how the concept of grace works in our everyday lives. It's a doctrine I think we members of the Church often misunderstand.

For instance, one day I was scrolling through Mormon.org and found a question asking what Mormons believe about the doctrine of grace. As I read through the different answers posted by Church members, I noticed that many mentioned 2 Nephi 25:23: "For we know that it is by grace that we are saved, after all we can do." Although there are over two hundred verses on grace in the standard works (and more than fifty of those in the Book of Mormon and Doctrine and Covenants), again and again Nephi's verse was the most often quoted. And many people interpreted that scripture by saying something like, in order to be saved, we must first do all we can on our own, and then Christ will make up the difference. "After" all our best efforts, they said, the Lord's grace will make up the rest.

But when Nephi said we're saved by grace "after all we can do," was he really saying we must work as hard as we can on our own and then Christ's grace will take us the rest of the way? Is that really how our Prince saves us? Is that really what is taught in the pages of the scriptures? After many years of studying this question, I'd like to suggest that our Prince would actually interpret Nephi's scripture differently.

To illustrate, let me show you a few additional scriptures—scriptures I believe we often overlook because we're so busy quoting 2 Nephi 25:23. I think once you've heard them, you'll begin to see Nephi's verse in a whole new light. The first one comes, surprisingly, from Jesus's own mouth. In John 15, He tells His disciples,

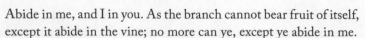
Abide in me, and I in you. As the branch cannot bear fruit of itself, except it abide in the vine; no more can ye, except ye abide in me.

I am the vine, ye are the branches: He that abideth in me, and I in him, the same bringeth forth much fruit: *for without me ye can do nothing.*" (John 15:4–5; emphasis added)

What did Jesus just tell us in these verses? Did it sound anything like, "Do your best, and I'll make up the difference"? Nope. Instead, the Lord said we can do *nothing* without His sustaining grace. After all, that's what happens when you turn into a dragon. There's *nothing* you can do on your own to change or improve your awful situation.

Let's continue with Jesus's vine and branch analogy by imagining that your parents are trimming the trees in your backyard. I want you to picture the pile of cut branches lying on the ground once they've finished their work. Tell me, can those branches grow any leaves on their own? Can they produce even one tiny piece of fruit? Can they decide to spring back to life while lying helplessly on the grass? The answer, of course, is no. That's because the branches are *dead*, and unfortunately, all they can do is *stay dead*.

As hard as it may be to hear, the same thing is true of you and me. We're spiritually dead, and on our own we can't do anything but *stay* spiritually dead. We can't grow green leaves or delicious fruit in our life—at least not without the grace of Jesus Christ.

The problem with saying that we must do our best and Christ's grace will make up the difference is that we're assuming there are a lot of good things we can do apart from Him and that we only need His help when we mess up or when we run out of steam. But that's not what Jesus taught at all, and it's not what Moroni said in the Book of Mormon either. Listen carefully to the prophet's words: "But behold, . . . every thing which inviteth and enticeth to do good, and to love God, and to serve him, is inspired of God . . . [for] *all things which are good cometh of Christ; otherwise men were fallen, and there could be no good thing come unto them*" (Moroni 7:13, 24; emphasis added).

I hope you didn't miss that last phrase. According to Moroni, being fallen has some unpleasant side effects, and one of them seems to be that we can't do any good on our own. He says that if any good works show up in our lives, it's only through the power of Christ that we've been able to do them. That's why he tells us our only hope is to "[rely] *alone* upon the merits of Christ, who [is] the author and the finisher of [our] faith" (Moroni 6:4; emphasis added). Notice, we don't rely on our own strength and our own merits for a while and then when that gives out, turn to Christ for help to do the rest. That would be like the dead branches trying to grow the first few pieces of fruit on their own. No, as a dragon or natural man, our only chance for redemption is by connecting with Christ's grace right from the start.

I absolutely love how LDS author Sheri Dew explains it:

> If we think we have to conquer a bad habit or an addiction by ourselves, before we seek help, we most likely don't understand grace. If we're discouraged with ourselves because we feel weak and succumb too readily and too often to temptation, we don't understand grace. . . . If we keep trying to suppress envy or anger that rises up at the worst moments, if we feel as though nothing ever changes and we can't seem to get over unfairness of hurt, if we feel unworthy of the Lord's help, we don't understand grace. . . . In other words, if we feel as though we're alone and must rely largely or even solely upon our own energy, talent, and strength— we don't understand grace. Or better said, we don't understand the enabling power of Jesus Christ.[2]

So if it really is true that we can do nothing without the Lord's help, then why did Nephi say we're saved by grace "after all we can do"? Perhaps it will help if I tell you that, in the Book of Mormon, the Anti-Nephi-Lehies said it was *all that [they] could do . . . to repent of all [their] sins* (Alma 24:11; emphasis added). It just so happens that the word *repent* in the Bible is often translated from the Hebrew word *sub*, which literally means "to turn to."[3] So the Lamanites were saying that all they could do was turn to their precious Redeemer for the grace needed to save them. And in the end, that's all we can do too. As prisoners in the dragon's lair, all we can do is turn to the one with the power to save us and redeem us. To put it a little more poetically, all we can do is run into the arms of our wonderful Prince.

So in this scene of the story, your goal is to stop trying to muster up your own willpower, stop making yourself promises you can't keep, and stop trying to be good all by yourself. Those efforts will never get you anywhere. You'll be just like the dead branches lying on the grass in your backyard, trying to grow fruit when you have no power to do so. The only way you'll ever change is by reaching for the supernatural grace of Christ. Just like Cinderella needed a fairy godmother, you need the power of your Prince in order to cast off your dragon rags and replace them with the gown of a royal princess. In the words of the prophet Jacob, "Redemption cometh in and through the Holy Messiah; for he is full of grace and truth" (2 Nephi 2:6).

The next thing we need to figure out is how we gain access to our Prince's grace. Thankfully, Cinderella's story will again give us a clue. Think back over the storyline of the movie and tell me: When, exactly, did Cinderella's fairy godmother choose to show up? It was at a powerful moment—the moment when Cinderella realized she'd completely run out of options. If you remember, after her stepsisters destroyed the dress the animals made, Cinderella ran out to the garden and collapsed to the ground in sobs. But the important thing wasn't that she was crying—the important thing was that she'd finally recognized that she could never free herself from her miserable life in bondage. Cinderella illustrated this when she said, "It's just no use. No use at all." That was the moment everything began to change for the desperate young woman.

In this scene of our princess story, it's time for you to come to the same point as Cinderella in the garden. It's time for you to "offer a sacrifice unto the Lord . . . of a *broken heart and a contrite spirit*" (D&C 59:8). But please don't think that just means you feel sad and dejected and all you can do is cry. We're going to look at a broken heart and contrite spirit much differently than that. For our purposes, having a broken heart means admitting once and for all that you're fallen and spiritually dead, and you can't do anything to change that. It means confessing (both to yourself and to your Prince) that you can't even get yourself partway out of the lair—that you really are in a "lost and . . . fallen state, and ever [will] be save [you] should rely on [your] Redeemer" (1 Nephi 10:6). Like Cinderella, those with a broken heart and contrite spirit admit that it's "no use at all" without the grace of Jesus Christ.

Believe it or not, a broken heart and a contrite spirit are things required of even the most righteous of Saints. Take the people of King Benjamin, for instance. In the first chapter of Mosiah, these people are described as "diligent . . . in keeping the commandments" and a "highly favored people of the Lord" (Mosiah 1:11, 13). Yet as amazing as this group may have been, once King Benjamin taught them about their natural man and how salvation can only come through Christ (Mosiah 3), the entire congregation "[fell] to the earth, for the fear of the Lord had come upon them" (Mosiah 4:1).

Why would such righteous people drop their faces to the dirt? It's because they "viewed themselves in their own carnal state, even less than the dust of the earth" (Mosiah 4:2). In other words, King Benjamin's people finally came face-to-face with their dragon skin in all its ugliness and sinfulness. In their desperation, they offered the Lord a broken heart and a contrite spirit by crying out in unison, "O have mercy, and apply the atoning blood of Christ that we may receive forgiveness of our sins, and our hearts may be purified; for we believe in Jesus Christ, the Son of God, . . . who shall come down among the children of men" (Mosiah 4:2). It was a powerful moment that brought incredible blessings to the lives of both King Benjamin and his people.

In another example, consider what Nephi did when he came face-to-face with his own dragon skin. (Remember when he said, "O wretched man that I am" in 2 Nephi 4:17?) Did he make a million promises to do better, set new goals, or muster up more white-knuckle willpower to stop sinning? No. Instead, he offered a broken heart and contrite spirit by begging the Lord to help him break free from clutches of the enemy. Listen carefully to his cry:

> O Lord, wilt thou redeem my soul? Wilt thou deliver me out of the hands of mine enemies? Wilt thou make me that I may shake at the appearance of sin?

May the gates of hell be shut continually before me, *because that my heart is broken and my spirit is contrite*! . . .

O Lord, I have trusted in thee, and I will trust in thee forever. . . .

Yea, I will cry unto thee, my God, the rock of my righteousness. (2 Nephi 4:31–32, 34–35)

I hope you can see that what your Prince wants most in this scene is not for you to try harder to be good, but for you to humble yourself before Him and tell Him how much you need Him. Like Cinderella in the garden, you display a broken heart and contrite spirit by falling to your knees and pouring your heart out to your precious Savior. Acknowledge that you just can't do it on your own. Tell Him that no matter how often you go to church, read your scriptures, or say your prayers, it will never be enough. It's only through His mercy and grace that you'll be able to return to your life as a royal princess.

That's exactly what Alma the Younger did in the Book of Mormon. He said, "Never, until I did cry out unto the Lord Jesus Christ for mercy, did I receive a remission of my sins. But behold, I did cry unto him and I did find peace to my soul" (Alma 38:8; see also Alma 36:18–21). I truly believe that crying out to our Prince like those in the Book of Mormon is the best way we can display a broken heart and a contrite spirit. This type of prayer doesn't have to be proper, fancy, or filled with impressive words and religious phrases. Instead, we can simply cry out from the depths of our souls and let our Prince know how urgently we need Him and His incomparable grace. And we can do it with confidence, knowing that "the Lord is nigh unto them that are of a broken heart; and saveth such as be of a contrite spirit" (Psalm 34:18).

You may wonder why in the world having a broken heart is so important. It's simple, really. If we remain unbroken (meaning we continue to think we can save ourselves by trying harder to live the Church standards or by keeping the commandments through our own willpower), we'll never allow Christ to lead us out of the dark and dreary dungeon. Instead, we'll just keep trying on our own to free ourselves from the awful monster.

To illustrate, imagine that instead of a cave, the dragon's lair is actually a complex and confusing labyrinth. Now picture yourself locked in a cell right smack in the middle of the maze. Suddenly, the Prince bursts into your cell, grabs you by the shoulders, and looks you squarely in the eyes. He tells you He can get you safely out of the lair, but the only way He can get you out is if you let Him do things *His way*. In other words, to make it out of the labyrinth safely, you can't tell Him what a great maze runner you are or make up your own plan and go the direction you think will be best. No, in order to outwit the villain (who will be doing all he can to keep you trapped in the lair), you must do whatever your experienced guide tells you to do the minute He tells you to do it. You must turn when He says turn, stop when He says stop, and run when He says run. It's the only way you'll ever find your way to lasting freedom.

Another example that illustrates this is a horse trainer who's trying to break a young colt. As long as the horse bucks, kicks, and tries to do things his way, the trainer won't be able to do anything with the feisty animal. But once the horse is truly *broken*, meaning it has given up its will to the will of its master, then the horse will finally work as one with its trainer. Elder Bruce D. Porter of the Seventy made this same point in the October 2007 general conference:

> Those who have a broken heart and a contrite spirit are willing to do anything and everything that God asks of them, without resistance or resentment. We cease doing things our way and learn to do them God's way instead. In such a condition of submissiveness, the Atonement can take effect and true repentance can occur.[4]

Did you notice how Elder Porter said a broken heart is what will finally allow "true repentance [to] occur"? Believe it or not, that's exactly where we're headed: right back to the topic of repentance. We've been talking about it for the last several scenes, but we still haven't really mastered it. And going through the repentance process is a crucial part of our personal princess story.

In a 1981 *Ensign* article, Elder Gerald N. Lund used a little analogy that can help us understand why this is so. In the article, he compared each of us to a powerhouse. It's the part of a dam that generates the power or electricity. Here's how Elder Lund explained the powerhouse's role:

> The powerhouse has no power residing in itself; the potential power rests in the energy of the river. When that source of power flows through the generators of the power plant, power is transferred from the river to the power plant and sent out into the homes (lives) of others. So it is with faith. The power . . . does not reside in man. Man requires the power of the atonement of Christ flowing into him. If no power is being generated, one does not—indeed, cannot—turn the generators by hand; . . . but rather, an effort [must be] made to remove those things which have blocked the power from flowing into the generators.[5]

Can you see that the powerhouse is just like one of those dead branches lying in your backyard? On its own, it has absolutely no power to do anything. But once it opens itself to the power of the river, the strong current begins to flow through the powerhouse in great abundance. Check out this picture of what can happen once the powerhouse is fully connected with the energy of the river. The results are pretty spectacular if you ask me.

I hope you also noticed something else Elder Lund said. The only way the powerhouse can open itself to the energy of the river is by *removing what blocks the water from flowing into the generators*. And that sums up the next scene in our princess story. Now that we've come to our Prince with a broken heart and contrite spirit, the next thing we need to do is repent—or remove anything and everything that blocks His grace from flowing freely into our hearts and lives. While this next scene won't be an easy one, it's the point where everything will finally begin to change. I promise you, through the repentance process, your Savior will slowly begin peeling off your dragon skin one small scale at a time.

For Additional Study

If you've spent many years frustrated by your weakness and discouraged by your inability to change on our own, read Ether 12:27 and then pay attention to President Ezra Taft Benson's commentary on that wonderful little verse:

> What a promise from the Lord! The very source of our troubles can be changed, molded, and formed into a strength and a source of power. This promise is repeated in one form or another in many other scriptures. Isaiah said, "He giveth power to the faint; and to them that have no might he increaseth strength." Paul was told by the Lord, "My grace is sufficient for thee: for my strength is made perfect in weakness." In the Doctrine and Covenants we read, "He that trembleth under my power shall be made strong, and shall bring forth fruits of praise and wisdom."
>
> Brothers and sisters, we must take our sins to the Lord in humble and sorrowful repentance. We must plead with Him for power to overcome them. The promises are sure. He will come to our aid. We will find the power to change our lives.[6]

If you want to read a powerful article on grace and how it works in our everyday lives, look up "His Grace Is Sufficient" by Brad Wilcox. (It's in the September 2013 *Ensign*). I love how Brother Wilcox again debunks the myth that grace only saves us after we work as hard as we can on our own. Here's how he explains it:

Grace is not a booster engine that kicks in once our fuel supply is exhausted. Rather, it is our constant energy source. It is not the light at the end of the tunnel but the light that moves us through the tunnel. Grace is not achieved somewhere down the road. It is received right here and right now.[7]

Now that you've had some time to ponder the Lord's grace and the importance of offering Him a broken heart and a contrite spirit, I want you to pull out your journal and write about how you can know if your heart is truly broken. One way you can tell is by answering the following questions: What do I do when I'm confronted with my personal sins and weaknesses? Do I make excuses? Rationalize my behavior? Justify my actions? Live in denial? Blame others? Try to cover it up? Or like Nephi in 2 Nephi 4, am I willing to acknowledge my true condition and admit my spiritual need before the Lord? Ponder and pray about what you can do to truly offer the Lord a broken heart and a contrite spirit just like those in the scriptures.

A CLOSER LOOK

ONE OF THE most wonderful things about the Book of Mormon is that we encounter many different people who've been set free from the dragon's lair. They're no longer dragons because they've been cleansed and purified through the Lord's precious Atonement. And when these people talk about repentance, one of the most important things they say is that they've received a *remission* of their sins. For instance, Enos made it clear that he "received a *remission* of [his] sins" (Enos 1:2; emphasis added). Samuel the Lamanite boldly proclaimed, "If ye believe on [Christ's] name ye will repent of all your sins, that thereby ye may have a *remission* of them through his merits" (Helaman 14:13; emphasis added). And when Benjamin's people cried out to the Lord, he says what they were actually doing was "begging for a *remission* of [their] sins" (Mosiah 4:20; emphasis added).

Have you ever thought much about the word *remission*? One way to look at it is to think about someone whose cancer goes into remission. When a doctor gives a patient that diagnosis, he's saying their cancer is gone, right? In other words, it's no longer spreading through their body and they no longer have to suffer from the symptoms of that dreadful disease.

In order for you to truly overcome the power of the enemy, the same thing must happen to you. You must repent so fully that your sins finally go into remission. You can't just keep going through the sin-repent-sin-repent cycle where you never really change and you never really overcome your same old sinful habits. That would be like the cancer patient continually going through chemo without ever getting any better. No, you must allow your Prince to remove your sins so fully that your dragon skin actually comes *all the way off.*

That's exactly what happened in the *Voyage of the Dawn Treader* when Eustace finally ran into Aslan, the great lion (in case you don't know, C. S. Lewis used the character of Aslan to represent Jesus Christ[1]). In that pivotal moment, Eustace finally stopped trying to pull off his dragon skin by himself and turned to the Great Lion to do the job instead. But it wasn't a painless process by any stretch of the imagination. Here's how Eustace describes it:

> The lion said, . . . 'You will have to let me undress you.' I was afraid of his claws, I can tell you, but I was pretty nearly desperate now. So I just lay flat down on my back to let him do it.
>
> The very first tear he made was so deep that I thought it had gone right into my heart. And when he began pulling the skin off, it hurt worse than anything I've ever felt. The only thing that made me able to bear it was just the pleasure of feeling the stuff peel off. . . .
>
> Well, he peeled the beastly stuff right off—just as I thought I'd done it myself the other three times, only they hadn't hurt—and there it was lying on the grass: only ever so much thicker, and darker, and more knobbly-looking than the others had been.[2]

Yes, it can definitely hurt to come face to face with our sin, or to let go of our favorite idols, or to confront the many lies we've been believing. So why in the world would we subject ourselves to such an uncomfortable experience? Why would we face it if it's going to be as difficult as Eustace said it was? We'll do it for the same reason Eustace did: because it will feel so good to see our dragon skin (or natural man) coming off. In the end, obtaining a remission of your sins won't just feel kind of nice or a little bit better—it will feel so amazing you'll hardly be able to find words to describe it!

Remember, King Benjamin said the remission of sins caused "exceeding great joy in [his people's] souls" (Mosiah 4:11). Not only that, but their "mouths [were] stopped that [they] could not find utterance, so exceedingly great was [their] joy" (verse 20). Tell me, have you ever felt such overpowering joy that it rendered you totally speechless? If not, prepare yourself, because that's exactly where we're headed in this part of our princess story. Though we'll face some difficult and perhaps even painful things in the upcoming scenes, just remember that the joy you'll receive when you obtain your own remission of sins will be greater than anything you've ever experienced.

Okay, to kick off this important scene, I want you to think back to the beginning of Eustace's tale. Do you remember the reason he turned into a dragon in the first place? It was because he gave in to the allure of the dragon treasure. In other words, as soon as Eustace succumbed to temptation, he ceased being a boy and began to turn into a rough and scaly monster.

Just like Eustace, we too have given in to temptation and believed the villain's lies. Because we've done this, dragon scales (or a natural man) formed on us as well. So the first thing we need to do is examine the different types of dragon scales that have wrapped themselves around our minds and hearts. Please note that we're not trying to peel off our sinful scales just yet. At this point, we're simply trying to understand what our dragon scales are made of so we can see the things our Prince must help us overcome. We'll do this by working our way through several commandments found in the scriptures. First I'll state the commandment, and then I'll give you some questions designed to help you evaluate the little ways you may be breaking that commandment in your everyday life. Finally, I'll ask you to go deeper and look for any lies you may be believing that are causing that sinful behavior.

It's just like that weed analogy we talked about earlier. Your outward sins are only the tops of the weeds; we need to look deeper so we can pull out the lies that are living at the root of each of those sins. As Elder Richard G. Scott has taught, "One can center his or her life in falsehood as though it were truth and be increasingly bound by the archenemy of God."[3] So in this scene, we're

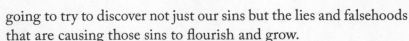
going to try to discover not just our sins but the lies and falsehoods that are causing those sins to flourish and grow.

Before we begin, let me remind you that the enemy has worked hard to blind you to his deceitful lies. As a result, many of the false beliefs living inside you will be difficult for you to see. For this reason, you need to work hand-in-hand with your Prince as you go through the following questions. Make sure to listen closely for any promptings and impressions the Lord brings to your heart and mind. That way, He'll be the true teacher as you examine your stubborn dragon scales one by one. Finally, don't forget to write down all those thoughts and impressions in a notebook or journal. (This is important!) In my own journal, I listed all the different sins that were weighing me down and keeping me in bondage, as well as the lies that were hiding underneath each of those sins. I did this so that when the time was right, I could tackle each individual sin—and the accompanying lies—with the help of my Prince. (I'll confess it was a pretty long list!)

All right, if you're ready to get started, take a deep breath and let's dive in.

Commandment One: "Thou shalt have no other God before me" (Mosiah 12:35; see also Genesis 35:2; Exodus 20:3; 2 Nephi 9:37; and D&C 1:16). This commandment goes back to the sin of idolatry we discussed in an earlier chapter. Remember, an idol can be anything we love or value more than God. It could be a person, a hobby, a goal, a priority, or even a deeply held dream. Like we've already talked about, some of your idols could include getting perfect grades, always having a boyfriend, being overly attached to media, or using food as a comfort or escape. Here are some questions you can ask yourself to see how you may have fallen victim to the personal sin of idolatry:

What do I turn to when I need to be renewed and recharged?

Is there anything in my life I've become obsessed with or addicted to?

What do I think I need to have in order to be happy?

Is there anything I can't live without?

Based on the things I do in my leisure time, what is the most important priority in my life?

Is the Prince my true treasure, or has something else (or a number of things) taken His place?

After pondering those questions, see if you can pinpoint the lies that have led you to turn to counterfeit gods. You probably never put these lies into words before, but that doesn't mean they're not still living deep in your heart. Here are a few sample lies to help get you thinking: "Social networking is harmless if it's only for a few hours every day," "If I can just be valedictorian, then I'll prove I'm worth something," or "Binging on chocolate is the perfect way to relieve my stress." Again, pray for help to see what lies are quietly fueling your personal idolatry and keeping you from offering your whole heart and soul to the Lord. Make sure to record all the thoughts and feelings that come as you do.

Commandment Two: "Thou shalt love thy neighbour as thyself" *(Mark 12:31; see also Luke 6:27–36 and 3 Nephi 12:38–44).* With this commandment, you get a chance to evaluate your relationships with others, especially the difficult people in your life. That includes family members, friends, peers at school, and even people in your ward. It also involves acquaintances you barely know and strangers you interact with from day to day. Here are some of the questions you need to consider to better understand this important commandment:

How do I treat my parents and siblings on a daily basis?

Have I ever spoken disrespectfully or rudely to someone?

Have I ever fought with someone or called that person names?

Do I gossip about any of my peers behind their back?

Do I tease or mock others in order to make the people around me laugh?

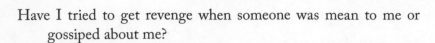

Have I tried to get revenge when someone was mean to me or gossiped about me?

How do I treat other people in general? Am I kind, patient, and compassionate, or impatient, curt, and sarcastic?

Have I ever prayed for help to love people I have a hard time getting along with? Or do I simply try to avoid them or ignore them?

After examining the ways you may be mistreating others, go a little deeper and look for the lies that may be causing you to act that way. Here are a few possibilities: "There's nothing wrong with sarcasm if they know I'm just kidding," "That person is just too weird or too hard to get along with," "My little brother is really annoying, so I just try avoid him as much as possible," or "It's not gossip; I'm just telling something that really happened." Allow your Prince to help you see how Satan has talked you into treating others in an un-Christlike way. Write down everything that comes to mind, even if it seems trivial or insignificant.

Commandment Three: "Look unto me in every thought; doubt not, fear not" (D&C 6:36; see also Deuteronomy 31:6; Luke 12:32; Mark 4:36–40; and D&C 38:15). It may seem odd that I'm including "fear not" as one of the Lord's most critical commandments. The reason I did is that every time you cultivate feelings of fear or doubt, you display a lack of faith in your Prince. The Apostle Paul said, "For God hath not given us the spirit of fear; but of power, and of love, and of a sound mind" (2 Timothy 1:7). So in those moments you're feeling a "spirit of fear," you can know for certain it's coming from the enemy.

Now, I know we live in a world where scary, awful, and difficult trials can happen to us (and probably already have). But the crazy thing about fear and anxiety is that we often end up stressing and worrying about things that never even come to pass! Thankfully, we can know that if they do, "the Lord thy God will hold [our] right hand, saying unto [us], *Fear not; I will help thee*" (Isaiah 41:13; emphasis added). Here are some questions to consider to see

if this dragon scale is one of the things you struggle with in your everyday life:

Do you live in fear of the future?

Do you constantly worry about bad things happening to you or to your family and how you will handle them?

Are you afraid to stand up for your values when others question them?

Do you worry that the Lord is going to ask you to do hard things if you submit your will to Him?

Do you ever lie awake at night, filled with anxiety over this problem or that concern?

Do you doubt that you'll ever see miracles in your everyday life?

Next, try to uncover the lies that are causing you to live with worry and fear. They may sound something like this: "I won't be able to survive if I lose someone I love," "Bad things always happen just when things are going good," "I can't handle the stress of that calling/assignment/move/mission," or "I'm afraid I'll never have anyone to rely on." I know thoughts like these often *feel* true because bad things *have* happened and people *have* let you down. But I promise you that once you learn to rely on your Prince, you'll overcome all fear and anxiety and live every single day in the light of the Lord. For now, your job is simply to let your Prince help you identify any false beliefs that are leading you to feel anxious, worried, nervous, apprehensive, or hopeless. Make sure to write down any impressions or promptings you feel as you pray about and ponder this particular subject.

Commandment Four: "*Continue in the spirit of meekness, and beware of pride*" (D&C 25:14; see also 2 Nephi 28:12; Mormon 8:36; Alma 38:11; and D&C 121:37). I know we often think of a prideful person as someone who is stuck up or conceited, but pride can actually display itself in a number of different ways. In a landmark talk in 1989, President Ezra Taft Benson explained pride like this:

Pride is a very misunderstood sin, and many are sinning in igno-
rance. In the scriptures there is no such thing as righteous pride—
it is always considered a sin. . . .

The central feature of pride is enmity—enmity toward God
and enmity toward our fellowmen. *Enmity* means "hatred toward,
hostility to, or a state of opposition." It is the power by which
Satan wishes to reign over us.

Pride is essentially competitive in nature. We pit our will
against God's. When we direct our pride toward God, it is in the
spirit of "my will and not thine be done."[4]

I'm sure you can think of plenty of times you followed your
own will instead of submitting to the will of the Lord. But to take
it even further than that, I want you to ask yourself these questions that target other areas of personal pride:

Am I a controlling person who has to get my way in every situation?

Do I have a hard time submitting to someone else's idea or plan?

Have I ever been disrespectful to teachers or leaders because I
thought what they told me to do was stupid?

How often do I ignore my prayers or scriptures in favor of doing
something that *I* want to do?

Am I mostly I focused on my own wants and needs, or do I consider the needs of others?

Do I brag about my own accomplishments to impress those around
me?

Do I dress or act a way to get attention from my peers?

As you answer each of these questions (and any others the
Spirit brings to mind), remember President Benson's counsel:
"Pride is a sin that can readily be seen in others but is rarely admit-
ted in ourselves."[5]

Obviously, there can be many different lies that cause us to
behave in a prideful way. These could include "My parents/lead-
ers/teachers don't know what they're talking about," "I'm only

voicing my opinion," or "I'm not showing off; I'm just sharing my talents." Record any lies you uncover as you continue to pray about the pervasive sin of pride in your life.

Commandment Five: "*I, the Lord, will forgive whom I will forgive, but of you it is required to forgive all men*" (*D&C 64:10; see also Matthew 18:21–35; Luke 6:37; 3 Nephi 13:14–15; and D&C 82:1*). This commandment is another tricky one because just like pride, grudges can be hard to see when they're hiding in our own hearts and minds. We may think we've forgiven others of all offenses against us, but there's a possibility that resentment or bitterness is still buried somewhere deep inside us. To uncover these sinful feelings, take some time to ponder the following questions:

Have I ever wanted to get back at people for something they did to me?

Do I hold a grudge against a family member, friend, teacher, or ward member?

Have I judged someone and continue to see the person in a critical light?

Do I blame other people for the bad things that have happened to me?

Do I feel even a small level of anger or bitterness for someone, even if it's for something that happened a long time ago?

Do I hold onto unkind feelings for *anyone* in my life?

You know what comes next. Try to uncover the lies lurking beneath all your uncharitable feelings. They may sound something like this: "What that person did was so terrible, I'll never be able to forgive them," "They don't deserve my forgiveness because they haven't apologized," or "It's not fair for me to be treated this way, so I shouldn't have to forgive them for what they did." Make sure to ask the Lord to show you any feelings of animosity you've been blinded to, and then try to capture those feelings the best you can in your journal. You may be surprised to find a nagging sense of

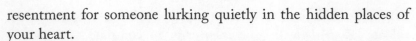

resentment for someone lurking quietly in the hidden places of your heart.

Commandment Six: "*Love not the world, neither the things that are in the world*" *(1 John 2:15; see also Luke 8:14; John 17:15–16; Colossians 3:2; and 3 Nephi 13:24).* This commandment is referring to the things, people, and activities in what Nephi calls the "great and spacious building" (1 Nephi 8:31). We each need to evaluate how heavily we're involved and even entangled with the things of the world. Now, I know we can't completely avoid worldly things, but the commandment above specifically mentions *loving* the things of the world, which means they've become our greatest joy and most important priority. Here are some questions that will help you decide how you're doing in this particular area of your life:

- Do I know more about celebrities or musicians (including the words of their songs and the details of their lives) than I do about the gospel?

- Have I become an obsessed fan, with pictures of that actor or band plastered all over my room, computer desktop, and phone?

- How do I decide what to wear or how much money to spend on clothes, makeup, shoes, and so on?

- Do I read gossip or teen magazines (or online articles) and try to follow their advice?

- Am I constantly trying to find a way to be more popular in the eyes of others?

- Do I measure my body size according to the standard of the world?

- On the Sabbath, is it hard for me to go without certain kinds of music and entertainment?

- How long can I last without seeing/watching/listening to the things of the world?

Once again it's time to go digging for the roots of these sins, or the lies Satan has convinced us to believe regarding worldly things. Here are some possible examples: "It's not breaking the Sabbath if I'm watching it or doing it with my family," "My music is edited so I can listen to it as much as I want," or "What can it hurt to follow my favorite celebrity's life?" When we believe lies like these, it's much easier to justify our worldly behavior. So our goal is to confront the root of our worldly habits, meaning our personal love of the world. Take some time to journal about how attached or devoted your heart is to the entertainment, clothing, hairstyles, sports, politics, or philosophies of today's culture.

Commandment Seven: "Cursed is he that putteth his trust in man, or maketh flesh his arm, or shall hearken unto the precepts of men" (2 Nephi 28:31; see also Jeremiah 17:5–8; Mosiah 23:14; D&C 5:21; and D&C 45:29). Next we need to talk about where we place our trust and whose counsel we choose to follow. In this generation, we have endless amounts of information at our fingertips, but that's not always a good thing. As President Dieter F. Uchtdorf has taught,

> Never in the history of the world have we had easier access to more information—some of it true, some of it false, and much of it partially true. . . .
>
> Part of our problem in the quest for truth is that human wisdom has disappointed us so often. We have so many examples of things that mankind once "knew" were true but have since been proven false. . . .
>
> It is always good to keep in mind, just because something is printed on paper, appears on the Internet, is frequently repeated, or has a powerful group of followers doesn't make it true.[6]

Just like President Uchtdorf said, we're constantly barraged with a flurry of worldly theories, ideas, attitudes, and philosophies. Even though others aren't always lying to us and trying to deceive us, it certainly could be happening. Nephi prophesied that even the "humble followers of Christ . . . [will] err because they are taught by the precepts of men" (2 Nephi 28:14). So we need to decide how we're handling the "precepts of men" whenever we encounter them. Here are some questions to consider:

Do I turn first to worldly sources (like my smart phone) for answers to my questions and solutions to my problems?

Do I follow any advice given in a TV show, Internet article, or book someone recommended without first praying and asking if the things being suggested are actually true?

Have I developed a habit of trusting everything I hear, or do I use the Spirit to help me evaluate the different philosophies that are being shouted at me from every direction?

Do I accept worldly ideas and theories as true simply because someone is an "expert"? (Remember, President Uchtorf just reminded us that many of those so-called experts—doctors, lawyers, scientists—have been proven wrong in the past.)

With the help of the Lord, do I really know how to recognize a "precept of men" when I hear one?

After pondering those questions, again take time to seek out the lies that may exist in this particular area of your life. They could sound like this: "I'm smart enough to figure things out on my own," "I can always look it up online," "I got an education for a reason," or "That person has a degree so they must be right." Try to figure out how Satan keeps you from looking to the Lord as your most important resource for guidance and direction. Watch yourself carefully the next time you have a question or a problem, and then journal about what sources you turn to in order to find answers.

Commandment Eight: "Thou shalt not covet" (Romans 7:7; see also Exodus 20:17; Luke 12:15; D&C 56:17; and D&C 88:123). I'm going to let President Gordon B. Hinckley describe the sin of covetousness because he captured it perfectly in a 1990 *Ensign* article:

> I wish to discuss a trap that can destroy any of us in our search for joy and happiness. It is that devious, sinister, evil influence that says, "What I have is not enough. I must have more.". . .
>
> I have observed that there are many in our present generation who with careful design set out on a course to get rich while still young, to drive fancy automobiles, to wear the best of clothing,

to have an apartment in the city and a house in the country—all of these, and more. This is the total end for which they live, and for some the means by which they get there is unimportant in terms of ethics and morality. They covet that which others have, and selfishness and even greed are all a part of their process of acquisitiveness.[7]

In a nutshell, to covet is to want something someone else has. It involves the sin of ingratitude (not being thankful for what you've already been blessed with) and also the sin of greed (being consumed with getting more). When we covet, we're saying that the Lord hasn't been as good to us as He's been to someone else, or that we need more this or that. Here are a few questions you can ask yourself with regard to the sin of covetousness:

Have you ever wished you could trade places with someone else—that you could have their life instead of yours?

Have you ever been obsessed with buying something one of your friends has?

Has a TV commercial or Internet ad convinced you that you just had to have something in order to be happy?

Have you ever been jealous of someone else's clothes, body, boyfriend, phone, house, intellect, or popularity?

In what ways do you forget about your blessings and instead hunger for more than what you've been given?

As usual, you next need to identify the lies that are lying at the root of these sins and quietly causing you to covet. Here are some sample lies to get you started: "If I lived in a bigger house, my life wouldn't be so stressful," "It's perfectly okay to spend my life pursuing the American dream," or "All my problems come because our family doesn't have enough money." Pray to be able to see any other lies that keep you from being content with the blessings the Lord has given you and write down any answers or insights that come through the power of the Spirit.

Commandment Nine: "Thou shalt not idle away thy time" (D&C 60:13; see also 2 Nephi 9:27; Alma 38:12; D&C 42:42; and D&C 88:69). I'm sure you know that being idle means wasting time and doing nothing—at least, nothing of any value. It means you're taking all the things the Lord has given you (energy, time, ability) and setting them aside in order to indulge your natural man. It may help to know that synonyms for *idle* include *empty, unproductive, frivolous, trivial, irrelevant,* and *unnecessary.*[8] As a mom of teenagers (and because I used to be a teenager myself), I know this commandment hits close to home for many in the younger generation. Here are the questions you can ponder on this particular subject:

How much time each day do I spend in idleness?

Are there any activities I participate in that the Lord would possibly see as empty or frivolous?

Do I ever procrastinate important projects or assignments until the last minute?

Have I concluded that I need a certain amount of "downtime" (or idleness) in order to cope with daily life?

What do I think the difference is between true rest and idleness?

Am I sure the Lord approves of the ways I choose to relax? Or would He have me manage my time in a more productive way?

As for the lies that may be fueling your idleness, they can take many different forms. They may include "It doesn't matter when I get it done as long as I finish it," "Video games help my brain relax and recover for a few hours every day," or "It's only fair that I get some time to myself." As you look for the lies that justify your idleness, allow the Spirit to help you see the difference between being idle and experiencing the true "rest of the Lord" (Moroni 7:3). Make sure to write down everything you're learning about how your Prince wants you to spend your leisure time.

Commandment Ten: "*Ye must practice virtue and holiness before me continually*" *(D&C 46:33; see also Psalm 24:3–4; 1 Corinthians 6:19; Galatians 5:16; and D&C 121:45).* This is a commandment LDS youth hear a lot from the leaders of the Church—especially the virtue part. In *For the Strength of Youth,* Church talks, and youth videos, you're told again and again that you must keep the law of chastity and be clean before the Lord. However, as you evaluate how you've done in this area, remember that this law includes much more than just not having sex before marriage. There are many ways this sin can sneak into your life. For example:

Does everything I read (including romance novels) live up to the standard of chastity and virtue?

Do I choose fiction that causes me to become sexually excited? Have I become addicted to those types of books?

Do I struggle with lustful thoughts or let myself indulge in romantic fantasies?

Have I allowed thoughts of the opposite sex to consume me to the point where I think about boys constantly throughout the day?

Have I done anything in my life that might embarrass or disappoint my future husband if he knew I did it?

Lies regarding chastity can be tricky because celestial marriage is a good thing, so we may believe that constantly thinking about boys is preparing us for the day we'll get married for time and all eternity. But as we said earlier, romance still can't be allowed to become our false god. Here are some lies that may allow us to rationalize this kind of behavior: "As long as the romance is clean, there's nothing wrong with reading as many of those books as I want," "If it's only a fantasy in my mind, then I'm innocent of any sin" (see Matthew 5:28 on this one), or "We kept all our clothes on, so making out wasn't that big of a deal." There are many different levels to the sin of chastity, so make sure Satan's lies aren't allowing you to justify sinning on *any* level.

With that said, I think it's time to take a little break from our self-evaluation. I know that was a lot to take in all at once. If you read through this section rather quickly, what I'd actually like you to do next is to slow down and go back through this chapter more carefully over the next few days. Even better, you could take a full week or two on each commandment. As you work your way through each section, ask the Lord to show you things in your life you've never been able to see before—especially the "secret faults" you don't even realize are there (Psalm 19:12). You need to go back through this scene more slowly because it often takes time for our hidden sins to rise to the surface. As you write down everything you're thinking and feeling in your journal (and I mean *absolutely everything*), I think you'll be surprised like Eustace at how thick, dark, knobbly-looking your dragon skin really is.

As you're identifying your personal sins and writing them down in your journal, you also need to confess each sin to the Lord as He brings it to mind. To *confess* is "to own or admit as true."[9] That means it's time to let go of all your excuses, stop living in denial, and be brutally honest with yourself (and your Prince) about the sins that continue to plague your heart and clog your mind. The Lord knows about all of them anyway, so there's no better time than now to fall on your knees and confess it all to Him. It's only when "we confess our sins, [that] he is faithful and just to forgive us our sins, and to cleanse us from all unrighteousness" (1 John 1:9). Confession is a critical part of the repentance process.

If this particular scene has made you feel self-conscious, embarrassed, or uncomfortable, I want you to remember that your Prince loves you more than you can even imagine. His whole intent is to transform you into something incredibly beautiful, but He can only do that if you allow Him access to the deepest secrets hiding in the corners of your heart. It's critical that you let Him see all the thoughts and feelings you've kept tucked away from the outside world. Show Him all the hurt, pain, doubt, and fear you've stuffed deep down inside. I promise you'll feel His perfectly gentle touch as He begins to redeem and heal those broken places inside you. But this will only work if you're completely honest with

Him about *all* your sins. I'm begging you: don't hold back even one small part of your heart. Just picture yourself looking into His eyes and feeling His tremendous love for you, and soon you'll find the courage to face even your ugliest personal sins through His empowering grace.

This may sound weird, but it's just like when you have the stomach flu and you're fighting the need to throw up even though you know it will make you feel better. You may want to keep all your sin hidden inside because you fear that letting it all out will feel awful, humiliating, horrible, or depressing. But I'm here to tell you that you really will feel better once it all comes out. With all your sins finally out in the open, you and your Prince can then clean up the mess in the upcoming scenes of our story.

More than anything, you must understand that if you skip this step or don't take it seriously, your Prince won't be able to change you back into a royal princess. Like Abinadi said, as long as you remain in your carnal state, the villain will have "all power over [you]" and you'll never be transformed into the holy, sanctified young woman you were meant to become (Mosiah 16:5). The only way you can truly break free from your natural man is through Spirit-led, Christ-centered, soul-deep, no-holds barred repentance.

So be brave. Let your Prince uncover the sinful dragon roots that are hiding quietly inside you. I promise that He'll reassure you, encourage you, and pour out His love as you work your way through the repentance process. And I'll let you in on a little secret. This step is just the beginning of your personal transformation. In the next few scenes, you're going to learn how to stay clean and dragon-scale-free *for the rest of your life.* This is important because most of us have gone through the repentance cycle many times before, only we've never been able to stop our sins from coming back again and again. This time, however, we're going to be so changed and transformed by the power of our Prince that the enemy's temptations will no longer have any influence over our hearts and minds.

After all, that's what repentance really means. I already told you that *repent* can be translated in Hebrew as "turn," but I haven't shared with you my favorite definition of the word. In the New Testament, *repent* is actually translated from the Greek word *metanoeo*. Here's how Elder Russell M. Nelson explains this wonderful word:

> When Jesus said "repent," His disciples recorded that command in the Greek language with the verb *metanoeo*. This powerful word has great significance. In this word, the prefix *meta* means "change." The suffix relates to four important Greek terms: *nous*, meaning "the mind"; *gnosis*, meaning "knowledge"; *pneuma*, meaning "spirit"; and *pnoe*, meaning "breath." Thus, when Jesus said "repent," He asked us to change—to change our mind, knowledge, and spirit—even our breath.[10]

I hope you can see you're beginning a process that will eventually lead to a radical change in your mind and your heart just like Elder Nelson said. Believe me when I tell you that you really will become a "new creature" in Christ—one whose thoughts, feelings, and desires have been changed, renewed, and transformed (2 Corinthians 5:17; see also Mosiah 27:26). Through the Lord's grace, your mind and heart will finally be filled with light, truth, joy, and peace rather than lies, fear, impatience, or selfishness. So take your Prince's hand and let Him walk you through this scene one small step at a time. Along the way, continue to record everything in your journal until you feel Him nod His approval that your confession is complete. Only then will you be ready for the next scene of our princess story.

For Additional Study

I'm guessing you already know the list of commandments we just covered wasn't all-inclusive. That's why it's important to continue to ask for personal revelation to help you finish your self-evaluation. As the Psalmist prayed, so you can pray: "Search me, O God, and know my heart: try me, and know my thoughts" (Psalm 139:23). Ask the Lord to help you see anything we didn't talk about in this scene so you can be sure to fully complete the repentance process.

One way you can do that is by continuing to look as deep as you possibly can into your mind and heart. Don't worry so much about your outward actions, but concentrate on the motives, desires, and beliefs that live buried inside you. If you allow the Lord cleanse your inner man (your dragon nature), your outward actions will straighten out on their own. The Pharisees are a perfect example of those who refused to let the Lord look into their hearts. All they cared about was maintaining perfect religious behavior. Read Matthew 23 to hear the stinging rebuke Christ gave to this group of outwardly religious men so we can make sure the same thing doesn't happen to us.

Finally, I think it would be helpful to read a little more about why confession is such an important part of the repentance process. Go to "Confession" in the Topical Guide and look up any verses that stand out to you. Then journal how you feel about this important step of repentance, and identify ways you can more openly acknowledge your sins before the Lord in prayer.

A GREAT EXCHANGE

THIS PARTICULAR SCENE opens with you holding your journal in your hands. Take a minute to open it and skim through everything you wrote down in the privacy of its pages. I'm guessing that by now your journal is filled with an eye-opening amount of information about your personal dragon scales. Were you surprised at all the sinful baggage you've accumulated over the years? I know I was. Like Eustace, I found that my dragon skin was much thicker and uglier than I'd ever imagined it could be. There were so many areas in my life that needed deep and lasting repentance.

As beneficial as this process was for me, I'll admit that I faced an enormous problem as I thumbed through the entries in my journal. It's that the more I wrote about my personal sins, the more I experienced overwhelming feelings of guilt, shame, and embarrassment. If the same thing is happening to you, the good news is that this scene of our story will teach us how to overcome all the painful feelings that come as a result of the repentance process.

I believe one reason we feel so much guilt and shame over our sins is because we know we need to be clean and pure in order to return to our heavenly home, and right now we're definitely not (see Alma 11:37 and Moses 6:57). Thankfully, our Prince is going to help us fix that particular problem, but at this point you need to know there's another reason we can be haunted by reoccurring feelings of guilt and shame. And I'm sad to say that it again involves our evil enemy and his sneaky little sidekicks.

You see, even though the repentance process is a much-needed step in your personal transformation, whenever you take that kind of up-close-and-personal look at all the sin in your life, it gives the villain the perfect opportunity to mock you and ridicule you for all the terrible things you've done. Did you know the word *Satan* actually means "accuser" or "slanderer"?[1] An accuser is one who blames, attacks, and does all he can to find fault. And in this scene of the story, you can bet the villain is jumping at the chance to accuse you and make you feel unworthy of your Prince's love and attention.

When you start examining your shortcomings, the accuser's whispers start raging in your mind: *Just look at what a horrible person you are. Why in the world would the Lord love you? Why would He ever want to help you? You're a mess. Just give up. There's no hope. You'll never be able to change.* On and on it goes. Because your sins are so fresh in your mind, the villain and his servants will take this opportunity to sneer in your ear and try to condemn you for each one of your personal dragon scales. In fact, if you've allowed your Prince to help you look deep into the corners of your heart, you may have found some ugly things lurking there. Your enemy knows that, and he's going to do all he can to get you to give in to feelings of despair, depression, or even all-out hopelessness.

The most critical question we need to answer right now is this: How in the world can we overcome our feelings of guilt when we really are guilty of all that sin? Believe it or not, there is a way to do it. Your Prince is eager to show you how it works. More than anything, He wants to calm your heart and melt away all those awful feelings for good. And the way He'll do it is through the process of *justification*.

Justification—or being justified—can be a little hard to understand, so I want to spend a few minutes discussing what it means. I think the easiest way to capture it is with a little analogy. Pretend you're sitting in the courtroom of heaven and you're on trial before God for all the sins you outlined in your journal. The only way you can get out of being punished for your sins is by being *justified*, which means the judge will pronounce you not guilty. As Elder D. Todd Christofferson has said, "We may appropriately speak of one who is justified as pardoned, without sin, or guiltless."[2] Justification is that magical moment when all the evidence against you is thrown out and you're no longer condemned for the things you've done. If you ask me, nothing would feel as amazing as being found not guilty when we come face-to-face with our Father in Heaven.

But we still haven't answered the question I posed earlier: How can we be justified or found not guilty when we really *are* guilty of all that sin? Some well-meaning people may say we can earn our justification by recommitting ourselves to work harder and do all we can to keep the commandments. According to this theory, if we try hard enough and do enough good works, the good we do will outweigh the bad, and God will eventually proclaim us not guilty. But guess what the scriptures say about that? Things just don't work that way in the courtroom of heaven.

For starters, Paul says, "By the deeds of the law there shall no flesh be justified in [God's] sight" (Romans 3:20; see also Galatians 2:16, 3:11). And in the Book of Mormon, Lehi repeats almost the exact same thing: "By the law no flesh is justified; or, by the law men are cut off" (2 Nephi 2:5). So why can't we be justified by trying harder to keep God's law? Well, it's like a murderer promising to do hours of community service in exchange for the judge letting him out of his sentence. His good works will never be enough to make up for his crime. There's a price that must be paid for that murderer's sin, and unfortunately, the same thing goes for our personal sins. God's law requires a punishment for those sins, and no amount of good works, service, or obedience can ever undo that punishment. What's done is done, and there's nothing we can do to change that.

But don't panic, because this is the part where our princess story gets really great. Since we can't be justified by working harder to keep the commandments, our Prince has prepared another way to justify us in the eyes of our Father in Heaven. It's simple and incredibly beautiful at the same time. The Doctrine and Covenants tells us that "justification [comes] *through the grace of our Lord and Savior Jesus Christ*" (D&C 20:30; emphasis added). In other words, it's through our Prince's Atonement that we can be found blameless in the courtroom of heaven. In fact, the Joseph Smith Translation makes this point extra clear in Romans 3:24. There, Paul says we're "justified *freely* by his grace through the redemption that is in Christ Jesus" (Romans 3:24; emphasis added). But in the Joseph Smith Translation, the prophet changed the word *freely* to *only*. It just goes to show that it's *only* through our Prince that we can be justified or pronounced not guilty when we stand in that heavenly courtroom.

So if the villain (or accuser) has been blaming you, shaming you, and trying to make you feel guilty for all your sins, I want you to imagine your Prince rising to His feet as He prepares to defend you. He's about to take His miraculous grace and apply it to your desperate situation. Again, His courtroom argument is not going to be what most people expect. He's not going to tell the Judge, "Look at all the good this young woman has done. I think she's accomplished enough righteous works to earn her salvation." No, He's actually going to say something that may sound a little bit crazy. He's going to stand and boldly "declare *his* righteousness for the remission of [*your*] sins" (Romans 3:25; emphasis added). It's a pretty amazing defense, if you ask me.

In the Doctrine and Covenants, Jesus shows us exactly what His courtroom argument will sound like. It goes something like this:

> Listen to him who is the advocate with the Father, who is pleading your cause before him—
>
> Saying: Father, behold the sufferings and death of him who did no sin, in whom thou wast well pleased; behold the blood of thy Son which was shed, the blood of him whom thou gavest that thyself might be glorified;
>
> Wherefore, Father, spare these my brethren that believe on my name, that they may come unto me and have everlasting life. (D&C 45:3–5)

That is what the Atonement is all about. In essence, your Prince is saying, "Father, I've shed my own blood to pay for this young woman's sins. Because I've already suffered her punishment, please find her not guilty— not because of her works, *but because of me.*"

What Jesus is offering here is what Christians around the world like to call the Great Exchange. As we sit in the courtroom of heaven, condemned for our sin, Jesus Christ pleads our case by not only taking on the punishment for our sins but also offering us *His* righteousness in exchange for our dragon nature. I think it's the greatest gift anyone could ever give a soiled and sin-stained royal princess!

To illustrate how the Great Exchange works, let's go again to the words of the Apostle Paul. You probably know that before Paul was ever a great preacher or writer of the scriptures, he was named Saul and was one of the most devoted Pharisees on the planet. And remember, Pharisees were experts at keeping the law of Moses. Paul even said he was "blameless" when it came to "the righteousness which is in the law" (Philippians 3:6). That means he did absolutely everything a good Pharisee was supposed to do. If Saul were a Mormon today, he would be the shining star of the entire ward. He'd read his scriptures for hours, he'd do his home teaching on the first day of the month, and he'd never drink caffeine or see PG-13 movies. In the eyes of others, he'd be a saint—a perfect example of what we tend to think righteousness should look like.

But something happened to Saul when Jesus appeared to him on the road to Damascus. Suddenly, he saw that righteousness didn't come by keeping a bunch of outward rules, but it came by having a pure heart and a divine nature—something Saul knew he definitely *didn't* have. So the newly named Paul stopped trying to be justified by obeying every tiny detail in the law and instead began to hunger for the Great Exchange. Speaking of Christ, Paul said, "[I want to] be found *in him*, not having mine own righteousness, which is of the law, but that which is through the faith of Christ, *the righteousness which is of God by faith*" (Philippians 3:9; emphasis added).

After his conversion, Paul no longer cared about having his "own righteousness" that he'd earned through his good works. Instead, all he wanted was to be found *in Christ*—meaning he'd obtained "the righteousness which is *of God* by faith." In another Epistle, Paul actually called it the "gift of righteousness" and noted that "by the righteousness of one the free gift came upon all men unto justification of life" (Romans 5:17–18).

I hope you noticed in that verse that through the righteous of one (our Prince), we get the "free gift" of justification. It's a gift we desperately need because we've sinned and we're unclean in the sight of God. And we can never pay the price for those sins, even if we spend the rest of our lives doing all the righteous works we can possibly muster. As Isaiah says, "We are all as an unclean thing, and all our righteousnesses are as filthy rags" (Isaiah 64:6). Thankfully, our wonderful Prince is willing to defend us in the courtroom by taking on our punishment and by replacing our sins with His perfect righteousness—a righteousness so enduring and eternal that we'll never have to feel unworthy, unclean, or sinful ever again.

We know that Nephi understood the Great Exchange because in 2 Nephi 4, the prophet begged the Lord, "Wilt thou encircle me . . . in the robe of *thy* righteousness"? (2 Nephi 4:33; emphasis added). I love the metaphor Nephi uses. Just imagine having Christ's righteousness wrapped around your body like a warm, comforting robe. It's a priceless, incomparable gift—something we could never obtain on our own, but something we absolutely can't live without.

The best part about participating in the Great Exchange is that once we're covered in our Prince's righteousness, we'll finally be set free from all our guilt and shame. You may be thinking, *But how can that happen? I've done so many bad things. Isn't the Prince disappointed in me? Isn't He angry or upset about all those things I wrote down in my journal?* The beautiful answer, sweet princess, is no. As Paul says, "There is . . . *no condemnation* to them which are in Christ Jesus" (Romans 8:1; emphasis added). Or as the Apostle John put it, "For God sent not his Son into the world to condemn the world; but that the world through him might be saved" (John 3:17).

Picture me using a megaphone as I say this to you to make sure you hear it loud and clear: *Your Prince did not come to condemn you!* He has absolutely no interest in shaming you, lecturing you, or making you feel bad for all your sins. Like John said in that scripture, your Prince came to *save* you, not criticize you. More than anything, He longs to cover you with His righteousness and wash away all your feelings of guilt and shame. From the bottom of His heart, you need to know that He really does forgive you for every sinful or wicked thing you've ever done.

If you don't believe me, listen to the way He says it in the scriptures: "Yea, and as often as my people repent will I forgive them their trespasses against me" (Mosiah 26:30). And again: "Behold, he who has repented of his sins, the same is forgiven, and I, the Lord, remember them no more" (D&C 58:42). It's just like the woman accused of adultery in John 8. She really was guilty of that particular sin, for she'd been caught "in the very act" (John 8:4). But when Jesus spoke to the woman, He didn't rebuke her, lecture her, or get mad at her for messing up. As she bowed at His feet, He simply said, "Neither do I condemn thee: go, and sin no more" (John 8:11). I love how He didn't condemn her *even though she was guilty of a grievous sinful act.* That means He's not going to condemn you, either. He's your Savior, your Rescuer, your Healer, and your Deliverer. All He wants to do is exchange your sins for His glorious righteousness. In what courtroom in the world would you get a deal like that?

All right, the time has finally come for you to have your personal day in court. I want you to pick up your journal and thumb through it again, noting all the things you've struggled with and all the times you've given in to temptation and sin. Now I want you to turn to Christ and ask Him if you can participate in the Great Exchange. Ask Him to replace your sinfulness with His flawless righteousness. Like the Psalmist David, you too can cry out: "In thee, O Lord, do I put my trust; let me never be ashamed: deliver me in *thy* righteousness" (Psalm 31:1; emphasis added).

I believe such a cry brings a huge smile to the face of your Prince. He's justified many people in the scriptures, and now He's thrilled to be able to do the same thing for you. Wrapped snugly in the robe of your Prince's righteousness, your heart will sing out just like Isaiah:

I will greatly rejoice in the Lord, my soul shall be joyful in my God; for he hath clothed me with the garments of salvation, *he hath covered me with the robe of righteousness*, as a bridegroom decketh himself with ornaments, and as a bride adorneth herself with her jewels. (Isaiah 61:10; emphasis added)

That, royal princess, is what it means to be justified. It's something you can never earn on your own. It's a free gift your Prince is waiting to give you. I think it's one of the most miraculous parts of our Prince's gospel plan. In the words of Elder D. Todd Christofferson, "[Christ] removes our condemnation . . . [and we] are pardoned and placed in a condition of righteousness with Him. We become, like Him, without sin. . . . We are, in a word, justified."[3]

Perhaps you're thinking, *It can't be that easy. All I have to do is turn to Christ and all my guilt will be taken away? He takes my punishment and I'm completely off the hook? That can't be right—there must something I have to do to repay Him.* Actually, there *is* something you can do to repay your Prince for all He's done for you. *You can believe He's telling you the truth.*

For instance, you can *believe* that He really does take your sins and give you His righteousness in return. You can *believe* that His perfect righteousness is now your own and that your sins are "remembered no more." You can *believe* that because of your Prince, every time your Heavenly Father looks at you (His royal daughter who has rolled around in the mud and soiled her sparkling gown in all kinds of different ways), He now sees His precious Son's righteousness as *your* righteousness. In a nutshell, you can *believe* that justification really is through the grace of your beloved Savior and Redeemer, Jesus Christ.

Now that the luxurious robe of righteousness is snuggled warmly around your shoulders, I want you to imagine the courtroom attendant handing back your journal and telling you that you're free to go. If you're anything like me, such a tremendous gift will cause an overwhelming love for your Prince to explode deep in the recesses of your heart. Truly, we've never experienced a love like His. And the best part is, our fairy tale still isn't over. There's much more waiting to be discovered. Hold on tight, because we're

about to move on to the next scene of this wonderful and miraculous princess story.

For Additional Study

I believe Romans is one of the most powerful books of scripture on the topic of justification. For instance, the word *justify* is mentioned thirty-one times in the New Testament, and ten of those are in the book of Romans. To see what I mean, read Romans 3 (including the chapter summary). Don't worry if you don't understand every word. Try looking up some of the cross-references to see if you can comprehend what Paul is trying to say. (Also, don't miss the Joseph Smith Translation additions in the footnotes. They really help to clarify Paul's message in this chapter!)

Once you have a feel for Paul's unique writing style, try moving on to Romans 9:30–32 and 10:1–4. If you're still having a hard time understanding what Paul is saying, ask a parent, leader, or seminary teacher to help you. Here Paul talks again about how our righteousness really does come from God and not from "the works of the law." Then finish off your study with the beautiful words found in Romans 5:1.

If you're interested in an inspiring little computer search, go to lds.org/scriptures and type "sins forgiven" into the search bar. There you'll find ninety different verses that will remind you of the Lord's desire to forgive your sins. Reading through scriptures like these can help it sink in that when you choose to repent, you really are completely and fully forgiven by your Prince.

If you're still having a hard time believing you can be forgiven (like you think the things you've done are just too bad for the Lord to wash away) consider the story of Alma the Younger and the sons of Mosiah. They were the "very vilest of sinners" (Mosiah 28:4), but they eventually became powerful men of God (see Alma 17:2–3). You'd think they'd never have been able to get over the guilt caused by all the horrible things they did, but these men learned for themselves about the power of the Lord's precious Atonement. To illustrate, read through Mosiah 27 and Alma 26.

What lessons can you learn from these men who truly knew in their hearts that they were forgiven?

A BAPTISM OF FIRE

I HOPE YOUR HEART is leaping and dancing over the wondrous gift you've just been given. It really is almost too good to be true. Not only has your Prince forgiven every single sin you listed in your journal (and even the ones that you forgot or left out!), but He's also clothed you with His perfect, enduring righteousness. As a result, you no longer stand condemned before God for your sinful thoughts, feelings, and behavior. For a fallen and sin-stained princess, I'd say this gift is more valuable than gold, diamonds, or pearls. It's the gift of *redemption*—and the amazing thing is, you've only received the *first part* of this incredible gift. We're about to uncover the next part in this scene of our princess story.

What more could you need than to be justified? Well, as wonderful as it is to be forgiven, you still face a really big problem. Though you left the courtroom a free woman, that awful dragon skin (or natural man) is still clinging to you. It's the root of all your sin, and it must be put off (Mosiah 3:19), or your sins will just keep coming back again and again. In addition to being justified, then, something more has to happen in order for you to be rid of your dragon skin for good. And that something is called *sanctification*.

Just in case you're a little fuzzy on the concept of sanctification, let me give you Elder Christofferson's simple definition: "To be sanctified through the blood of Christ is to become clean, pure,

and holy."[1] Alma describes sanctification when he tells us we must be "changed from [our] carnal and fallen state, to a state of righteousness, being redeemed of God, [thus] becoming his sons and daughters" (Mosiah 27:25). But I want to be clear we're not just talking about our *actions* becoming clean, pure, and holy. Sanctification means our *thoughts*, *feelings*, *motives*, *desires*, and *intentions* will be purified, cleansed, and made new. When that happens, we won't just see a radical change in our outward behavior—we'll actually experience a "mighty change" deep inside our hearts (Alma 5:14).

Another important thing you need to know about sanctification is that, just like justification, it can't be earned. Like I keep saying, you can't get it by working harder, exerting more willpower, or setting a bunch of new goals. No, the Doctrine and Covenants makes it clear that "sanctification [is] *through the grace of our Lord and Savior Jesus Christ*," just like justification (D&C 20:31; emphasis added). Moroni echoed the same idea when he said, "Ye [are] sanctified in Christ by the grace of God, through the shedding of the blood of Christ" (Moroni 10:33). Put simply, Christ's grace justifies us, and Christ's grace will also sanctify us, for as the Prince Himself reminds us, "*I* am able to make you holy" (D&C 60:7; emphasis added).

I love how Elder Christofferson calls both justification and sanctification "gift[s] of grace." He continues,

> It is not that we *earn* these gifts, but rather that we choose to seek and accept justification and sanctification. . . . This action of acceptance on our part opens the door for the process of justification (remission, or pardoning, of sins) and sanctification (cleansing from sin) to work in us—something we may refer to as being born again.[2]

We've finally reached one of the most wonderful parts of our princess story. In this scene, we get to talk about being born again. It's one of my favorite subjects in the whole wide world. That's because when you're born again, the old you (meaning your natural man or that annoying dragon skin) actually *dies* and you're spiritually reborn as a new person. The scriptures even say that the new you will have "no more disposition to do evil, but to do good continually" (Mosiah 5:2). Can you imagine what it would feel like to lose all desire for sin? Can you imagine having a heart so cleansed and purified that you feel, think, and act like a completely different person? This is definitely a part of the story you don't want to miss.

Being sanctified or born again is such an overwhelming change that you may wonder how it can ever happen to you. The "how" is actually a really amazing process. It comes through the grace of Christ, but there's a little more to it than that. I think the best way we can understand it is by going back to our Prince's strategy to save us—the strategy He calls His gospel. Let's quickly review the first principles and ordinances of that gospel as listed in the fourth article of faith.

As you already know, the first principle is faith in the Lord Jesus Christ, and the second one is repentance (we've already talked a lot about both of those). The third one is baptism by immersion, which I'm guessing you've already experienced (if you haven't, maybe it's time to give the LDS missionaries a call!). All we have left is the fourth principle of the gospel, which is receiving the gift of the Holy Ghost by the laying on of hands. However, if you think you already know everything there is to know about the Holy Ghost, think again.

I know most of us have probably been taught a lot about the Holy Ghost in Primary, Young Women, seminary, family home evening, and general conference. But I still think we often underestimate what the gift of the Holy Ghost is all about. Yes, He can comfort us, warn us of danger, and help us find things we've lost, but the Holy Ghost's role involves much more than that. Ultimately, this gift is given to us for one critical reason: so each of us can be "baptized with fire and with the Holy Ghost" (Ether 12:14). It's a different baptism than being immersed in water. This time you're immersed in your Prince's holy, cleansing fire, and the results will simply be spectacular.

Surprisingly, a great example of the transforming power of fire can be found in the Harry Potter series. If you're a Harry Potter fan, you know that Dumbledore had a wonderful pet bird named Fawkes, a phoenix. Fawkes had an unusual ability: he could die and automatically be reborn. But how did he die? The great bird burst into flames and then was magically born again from the ashes.[3] I believe the key to Fawkes's rebirth was actually in the fire. After all, think about all the things fire does. It burns away all dross and impurities. It transforms whatever it touches. It incinerates the old to make room for the new. Just like Fawkes was reborn out of the fire's ashes, so your natural man must also be incinerated to make room for the new you. And that right there is a perfect description of sanctification. Sanctification and the baptism of fire really are one and the same. As Elder Christofferson points out, "We may appropriately speak of sanctification as the baptism of the Spirit, or being 'baptized with fire, and with the Holy Ghost' (Moses 6:66)."[4]

Being baptized by fire is such a cool concept that we're going to explore in greater depth while we walk through this scene of our story. I think you'll like what Joseph Smith had to say about the baptism of fire and the Holy Ghost:

> You might as well baptize a bag of sand as a man, if not done in view of the remission of sins and getting of the Holy Ghost. *Baptism by water is but half a baptism, and is good for nothing without the other half—that is, the baptism of the Holy Ghost.*[5]

And Joseph isn't the only one who said something like that. Several times in the scriptures, the Lord Himself pointed out that the baptism of water must be followed by the baptism by fire—that holy fire is what will bring a remission of our sins. Here are just a few examples:

> For the gate by which ye should enter is repentance and baptism by water; *and then cometh a remission of your sins by fire and by the Holy Ghost.* (2 Nephi 31:17; emphasis added)

> Blessed are they who shall . . . come down into the depths of humility and be baptized, *for they shall be visited with fire and with the Holy Ghost, and shall receive a remission of their sins.* (3 Nephi 12:2; emphasis added)

For a final witness of this truth, consider the words of Elder Boyd K. Packer:

> We sometimes speak of baptism for the remission of sins. The remission, if you will read the scriptures carefully, comes through the baptism of fire and of the Holy Ghost.[6]

I'm going to repeat that one more time just to make sure it's drilled into your head: *The only way to get a remission of your sins is through the baptism of fire and the Holy Ghost*. It's a huge part of your personal princess story.

So that brings us right back to the question we posed earlier: How in the world can we be sanctified? To answer that, let's return to an analogy we used in an earlier scene. Remember how we tied the remission of our sins to someone's cancer going into remission? If you've had a loved one go through that awful disease, you probably know how they administer the chemotherapy. Most of the time, it's transmitted into the body through an IV in the patient's arm. The medicine goes through the IV and into the bloodstream, where it can then find and attack all of the dangerous cancer cells. But the part of the analogy I want to focus on is that the chemo first has to *get inside* the patient for it to work the way it should.

Believe it or not, the baptism of fire works the same way. In this example, the chemotherapy represents our Prince's grace, and the IV represents the Holy Ghost. Because the Holy Ghost can "dwell in you" (Romans 8:9), He's able to transmit Christ's grace to the deepest parts of your mind and heart. And what does this medicine do once it gets inside you? According to Elder David A. Bednar, "the Holy Ghost sanctifies and refines our souls as if by fire," and as a result, we receive "a fundamental change in our desires, our motives, and our natures made possible through the Atonement of Christ the Lord."[7] Pretty amazing cure if you ask me.

Because the baptism of fire is such a dramatic transformation, it's going to take us several scenes to not only understand it but also experience it in our individual lives. There are some specific steps we can take in this scene that will help get the process started. Elder Bednar outlined these steps in his 2007 general conference talk "Ye Must Be Born Again." Using the analogy of how a cucumber is turned into a pickle to represent spiritual rebirth, he noted that the "first basic steps in the process" are "proper preparing and cleaning."[8]

Just like Elder Bednar said, it's time for us to prepare and cleanse our lives by removing all the obstacles that keep our Prince's grace from flowing freely into our minds and hearts. Using our chemo example, our goal in this scene is to clear the way for the IV so the medicine of Christ's grace can get exactly where it needs to go.

One way we can prepare and cleanse ourselves is by making a list of all the sinful and distracting things in our lives that need to be chucked in the trash. That list could include inappropriate movies, TV shows, and music; immodest clothing; excess time on social media; or anything else that distracts our minds and drives away the Spirit. However, I must admit that I'm not really interested in taking that approach. You hear that advice all the time from parents and leaders in the Church. Even though it's right on target (and I've given that same advice to my own kids), this time I want you to look at this type of spiritual housecleaning in a new way. If I can help you understand *why* such a housecleaning is necessary, then perhaps you won't see it as a bunch of rules that take away the fun in your life, but instead as a way to draw closer to your precious Prince.

To illustrate, think back to that picture of the princess playing video games with the dragon. To me, the main problem in that picture wasn't that the princess was so heavily involved in the dragon world. It was that she'd *completely forgotten about her prince*. He'd come a long way to rescue her and save her from the clutches of the monster, and the true tragedy is that she didn't even care. For the princess, it was as if the prince didn't even exist.

So in the end, the spiritual housecleaning we're talking about has less to do with keeping a bunch of rules and more to do with turning away from anything that makes us forget or lose interest in our Prince. Jesus Christ wants (and deserves) our whole heart, not just a small part of it. That's the way relationships of love always work between two people. No man in his right mind would take a wife who keeps a few lovers on the side, so why should we expect our Prince to be any different? No, He really does insist on having all our soul and all our "heart, might, mind, and strength" (D&C 4:2). To give Him that gift, then, we must let go of anything that keeps us distracted, sidetracked, or separated from His glorious presence.

Leaving things behind for our Prince is a decision that all princesses face at one point or another. Take Kate Middleton for instance. The only way she could become a royal princess was by completely giving up her old life. She couldn't stay who she was and go with her prince. Instead, she had to sacrifice all her former comforts so she could step into a new world of castles and kings. And that's what your Prince is asking you to do. He wants to know if, like Kate, you're willing to give up all the old things that used to occupy your mind and heart so you can inherit the life of a future queen. I promise the payoff will be worth it.

A beautiful example of one who gave the Lord his all is found in Alma 22. Lamoni's father, the great Lamanite king, started off by asking Aaron an important question. He asked, "What shall I do that I may be born of God, having this wicked spirit rooted out of my breast?" (Alma 22:15). When Aaron told the king about the path to spiritual rebirth, the Lamanite leader immediately fell down to the earth and cried out, "O God, Aaron hath told me that there is a God; and if there is a God, and if thou art God, wilt thou make thyself known unto me, *and I will give away all my sins to know thee*" (Alma 22:18; emphasis added). Can you see that this passionate and powerful king was willing to give up *everything* he had for the blessing of being born again? He even proved it when he said, "I will give up all that I possess, yea, *I will forsake my kingdom*, that I may receive this great joy" (Alma 22:15; emphasis added).

So the questions you must ask yourself right now are these: Do I feel the same way about being born again? Am I also willing to "give away all my sins" so my Savior can change me? Am I willing to sacrifice anything that distracts, diverts, or tears me away from His precious presence? I'm hoping your answer to all three questions is a big, fat yes. I'm hoping you're so filled with love for your amazing Redeemer that you'll easily choose Him over the fleeting and shallow things of the world. It's the perfect way to show Him that He matters to you more than anything else in your entire life.

As you prepare to do this spiritual housecleaning, I need to warn you that this step may be more difficult than you think. I say that because cleaning out your music playlist or the clothes in your closet is much easier than cleaning the anger out of your heart, throwing the false gods out of your life, breaking free from an unyielding addiction, or letting go of a grudge you've held against someone who's hurt you. That's the reason you need the chemotherapy of your Prince's grace. Only He has enough strength and power to remove those dragon scales that have wound themselves so tightly around your mind and heart. So know this: even though the process of removing your sin starts in this scene, it's going to continue for several scenes as we learn how to access and internalize our Prince's enabling grace. But for now, let's go ahead and move on to the next step in the sanctification process.

Thankfully, Elder Bednar also described this second step in great detail. He said that after being scrubbed clean, a cucumber must be fully saturated in salt brine to become a pickle. He then tied it to our personal lives:

> After we come out of the waters of baptism, our souls need to be continuously immersed in and saturated with the truth and the light of the Savior's gospel. Sporadic and shallow dipping in the doctrine of Christ and partial participation in His restored Church cannot produce the spiritual transformation that enables us to walk in a newness of life.[9]

I think the key phrase in that passage is "continuously immersed in and saturated with," as opposed to "sporadic and shallow dipping." I believe Elder Bednar is talking about completely immersing and saturating ourselves in the kingdom of our Prince. It may help to know that some synonyms for the word *immerse* include *bathe*, *bury*, *douse*, *drench*, or *submerse*.[10] I like the definition even better: "to involve deeply" or "absorb."[11] So that means the only way for us to be baptized with fire and born again is to become not just involved but completely absorbed in the gospel of Jesus Christ.

Now, I'll admit that at first I was confused by this idea. How could I live my normal life with all its demands and still be deeply absorbed in the gospel? My day often included a lot of spiritual stuff like going to church, saying my prayers, and having family home evening, but I also had a lot of responsibilities pressing on me that didn't seem spiritual at all. Did being immersed in the gospel mean I had to give all that up and read my scriptures all day long? Did I have to listen to the Mormon Tabernacle Choir 24/7 and never watch TV again? It just didn't seem realistic when I had so much going on in my everyday life.

Thankfully, my Savior taught me that I was looking at this part of the process all wrong. Truth is, we all have lives to live, and those lives include a lot of ordinary things like washing dishes, running errands, doing homework, or babysitting. And those things may seem like they're keeping us from being absorbed in Jesus Christ, but that's not the case at all. In order to be "continuously immersed in and saturated with" our Prince's world like Elder Bednar said, we have to do only one thing: we must include the Lord in every part of our day, whether we're doing something Church-related or not. Alma paints a perfect picture of this kind of spiritual immersion and saturation:

> Yea, and cry unto God for all thy support; yea, let all thy doings be unto the Lord, and whithersoever thou goest let it be in the Lord; yea, let all thy thoughts be directed unto the Lord; yea, let the affections of thy heart be placed upon the Lord forever.
>
> Counsel with the Lord in all thy doings, and he will direct thee for good; yea, when thou liest down at night lie down unto the Lord, that he may watch over you in your sleep; and when thou risest in the morning let thy heart be full of thanks unto God; and if ye do these things, ye shall be lifted up at the last day. (Alma 37:36–37)

Did you hear Alma say that *all* your doings should be unto the Lord? And also *all* your thoughts and *everywhere* you choose to go? Right there is the immersion I believe Elder Bednar was talking about. Whether we're doing something religious (like a service project with our church group) or something not-so-religious (like cleaning the garage with our dad), we still have the power to

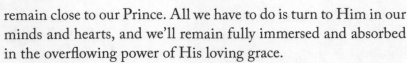

remain close to our Prince. All we have to do is turn to Him in our minds and hearts, and we'll remain fully immersed and absorbed in the overflowing power of His loving grace.

But there's much more to spiritual immersion than just keeping Christ by our side throughout the day. When we absorb and saturate ourselves in our Prince's power, we're not just including Him in our to-do list—we're actually *surrendering* that list (and our entire lives!) over to Him so that He may "rule and reign" over every single part of our existence (Helaman 12:6). After all, that's His right as our true "Eternal King" (D&C 128:23). To be clear, our goal isn't just to fit our Prince in somewhere between our busy social lives and our various activities. It's not about making room for Him on the shelf. I'm talking about giving Him the *whole* shelf, meaning we make Him Lord over every single area of our personal lives.

If that seems like an overwhelming undertaking, let me offer you a little encouragement. This step in the sanctification process is one of those things that happens "line upon line, precept upon precept," which means you don't have to get there all at once (D&C 98:12). Slowly, as you draw closer to the Lord and as you're more empowered by His enabling grace, you'll find that you're eager to surrender more of your life into His capable hands. That's exactly how the Nephites experienced it in the Book of Mormon:

> Nevertheless they did fast and pray oft, and did wax stronger and stronger in their humility, and firmer and firmer in the faith of Christ, unto the filling their souls with joy and consolation, yea, even to the purifying and the sanctification of their hearts, which sanctification cometh because of their yielding their hearts unto God. (Helaman 3:35)

I think it's cool that, over time, these people slowly got stronger and firmer in the faith of Christ. Even better, the more they "yield[ed] their hearts" to Him, the more their souls were filled with "joy and consolation." It's an incredibly beautiful progression that will bless your life in immeasurable ways. But it's okay to give yourself time for it to happen naturally. I promise that once you see the miracles the Lord can work in your everyday life,

you'll want to surrender every single part of yourself into His precious care—to truly "offer your whole [soul] as an offering unto him" (Omni 1:26). You'll want Him to reign over your education, your family time, your dating and social life, your future plans, your everyday responsibilities, and even your deepest dreams and desires. The more you surrender yourself into His hands, the more His grace will surge inside you and transform your life beyond anything you've ever imagined.

With that said, let's pause for a moment and take a look at where we've come so far. I'm pretty sure you understand the preparing and cleansing step, and you're also learning how to be saturated and immersed in the sweet presence of your Prince. That means the time has come to prepare for battle. *A fight scene?* you ask. Absolutely. Every princess story has an epic battle scene and your story is no different. So a big part of your training includes learning to defend yourself against the villain's powerful temptations. In fact, your Prince wants to teach you how to fight in such a way that you truly become a "conqueror; yea, that you may conquer Satan, and that you may escape the hands of the servants of Satan that do uphold his work" (D&C 10:5). It's the only way you'll ever truly be born again.

Just think: Finally you'll know how to overcome those annoying little temptations that continue to plague you from day to day. Finally you'll triumph all over the miserable sins and struggles you've recorded in your journal. Finally you'll know how to think and act like a princess instead of a horrible little monster. It's definitely a battle worth fighting, and with your Prince's help, you know you'll be able to win.

If you'll join me in the next scene of our story, the Prince is anxious to prepare you for the fight.

For Additional Study

One cleansing step I'd never thought much about (but in reality was quite difficult for me) was identifying all the idols or false gods I'd allowed into my life. At first I didn't think I worshipped any idols. But as I began to pray about it, the Lord showed me the many different things that meant much more to me than He did.

I never saw those things as false gods, but they really had captured a huge part of my heart. If you haven't thought much about idols either, here are a few resources to help you uncover where the counterfeit gods may be hiding in your personal life:

Spencer W. Kimball, "The False Gods We Worship," *Ensign*, June 1976. (I especially love the story of the monkey and the nut!)

Dennis Largey, "Refusing to Worship Today's Graven Images," *Ensign*, February 1994. (This one has a lot of ideas that young women can relate to.)

"The Other Six," *New Era*, August 2013. (See also Elder Perry's original talk where he talks quite a bit about idolatry but also mentions other commandments we often tend to struggle with: "Obedience to the Law Is Liberty," *Ensign*, April 2013.)

In 2 Nephi 31, Nephi says that when we're baptized by fire and the Holy Ghost, we "can speak with a new tongue, yea, even with the tongue of angels" (2 Nephi 31:14). What do you think that means? And why would it matter to you? (You can find a clue in 2 Nephi 32:2–3).

Since I used so many ideas from Elder Bednar's pickle talk, it would be wonderful for you to read and review the whole thing. His analogy is easy to understand and applies amazingly well to our individual lives. Again, the title is "Ye Must Be Born Again," and you can find it in the May 2008 *Ensign*.

A PRINCESS WARRIOR

DO YOU REMEMBER how the villain is conquered at the end of almost every princess movie? Most of the time, the princess doesn't sit back helplessly while the prince does all the work, does she? Instead, the two join together as a team to defeat the villain and his or her minions. Though the prince ultimately does the saving, the princess works with him in order to crush the villain and the evil sidekicks once and for all.

Just like the movie princesses, the time has come for you to join the fight. But the only way you can safely do that is by letting the Prince make you into a *princess warrior*. Don't act so surprised—princesses can be warriors too. In fact, each and every one of us was sent to this earth to stand as a valiant soldier alongside our Prince. I think the problem is that most of us have never really learned how to fight the enemy in such a way that we truly become victorious—not just for today but for the rest of our lives.

In order to prepare you for battle, I want to share something the Apostle Paul wrote that I believe will both inspire and motivate you to action: "The night is far spent, the day is at hand: let us therefore cast off the works of darkness, and let us put on the armour of light. . . . Put ye on the Lord Jesus Christ (Romans 13:12, 14).

The armor of light. It's a powerful image, don't you think? Did you notice that Paul also said, "Put ye on the Lord Jesus Christ"?

I think it's intriguing that he tells us to "put on" our Prince just like we put on the pieces of armor. In the end, the analogy works because it's Jesus Christ Himself who will be our armor and our strength as we battle the villain. The Lord said as much in the Doctrine and Covenants:

> Wherefore, I call upon the weak things of the world, those who are unlearned and despised, to thresh the nations by the power of my Spirit;
>
> And their arm shall be my arm, and I will be their shield and their buckler; and I will gird up their loins, and they shall fight manfully for me; and their enemies shall be under their feet; and I will let fall the sword in their behalf, and by the fire of mine indignation will I preserve them. (D&C 35:13–14)

Please don't miss this important point. When you strap on the armor of light, what you're really doing is *putting on Jesus Christ*, just like Paul said. In essence, each piece of armor is going to represent a part of the Lord's nature that He'll share with you so you can conquer the enemy. After all, it's the armor *of God*, not some metal suit you can scrape together on your own. So the only way you can obtain it is to receive it as a *gift* from your Savior and Redeemer. Keep that in mind as we discuss this wonderful armor, piece by piece. After we learn about each part, it will be time for you to suit up, and the battle will begin.

The armor of God is actually described two different times in the scriptures—once in Ephesians 6 and once in Doctrine and Covenants 27. Those two accounts (which are almost identical) tell us that the first thing we need to do is have "[our] loins girt about with truth" (D&C 27:16; Ephesians 6:14). In other words, we must wrap the belt of truth tightly around our center.

To understand this pivotal piece of a warrior's clothing, let's look a little deeper into the meaning of the word *truth*. Often we think of truth as a correct fact or principle (and it definitely is that), but I want to tweak it a little while we're talking about the armor of God. You may be surprised to learn that the word *true* is actually derived from an ancient word for tree, so it carries the meaning of being "steadfast as an oak."[1] That's why some of

the synonyms for *true* include *sincere*, *dependable*, *authentic*, and *trustworthy*.[2] So if we look at the belt of truth through this lens, we'll see that a warrior who's wearing this piece of armor is completely dedicated, devoted, and committed. He's as steady as an enormous oak tree, not one who will bend or break the minute the wind starts to blow. He's the kind of soldier you love to see in the movies—the kind you know will stay by your side no matter how bad the skirmish gets.

Obtaining this particular belt is a critical part of becoming a princess warrior. After all, how far will you get in the battle if your heart just isn't in it? If you're just going through the motions? If you're entering the conflict with a lukewarm attitude and a wavering sense of commitment? That's the last kind of soldier I'd want fighting by my side. And our Prince feels the same way. He needs a princess warrior who will be *true* to Him, who will be devoted and committed to His cause with all her heart and soul.

In the end, the belt of truth is really about *desire*. How badly do you really want to win this fight? Are you just going through the motions when it comes to spiritual things? Or are you really steadfast, committed, and devoted to your Prince? Does your motivation give out when the going gets tough? Or are you really *true* to your hero at all times, in all things, and in all places? While we all want to believe we're as steadfast as an oak, the truth is that our lives may be telling a different story.

Let's get real for just a minute. Don't we sometimes wake up and the *last* thing we feel is committed, devoted, or steadfast? On mornings like that, all we want to do is pull the covers up over our heads and avoid the battle altogether. We don't want to fight the enemy—we just want to play on our phones, talk to our friends, or spend a few hours lost in a good movie. So how do we kindle that flame of desire—that raging fire of commitment, devotion, and steadfastness—when we just aren't feeling it? The answer is simple: we must pray for it. Remember, the belt of truth represents a part of *Christ's* nature, not our own. We can't stitch together the ability to be true and steadfast all by ourselves. We're mortal, and we'll never have the resources to be that strong. Thankfully, we can ask our Prince for the densely woven and unwavering belt of truth.

Once it's wound carefully around our core, we'll feel our Savior's desire, commitment, and steadfastness becoming our own. It's the only way we'll ever be true in the heat of the moment when the enemy is coming at us with all the ammunition in his arsenal.

The Lord gave the belt of truth to the people of Alma when they were in bondage to the Lamanites. Because they asked Him (Mosiah 24:12), He blessed them with such a powerful sense of devotion and commitment that they were able to "submit cheerfully and with patience to all the will of the Lord" even though they were in an incredibly difficult situation (Mosiah 24:15). Satan and his sidekicks could not persuade them to whine, complain, or lose faith for even a minute. Why? Because their Redeemer had wrapped them tightly in the belt of truth. And He can do the same thing for you. If you'll let Him bind you firmly in this powerful belt, you too will find the strength to remain steadfast and devoted, even when you're facing the worst the enemy has to offer.

Okay, princess warrior, which piece of armor comes next? The scriptures call it the "breastplate of righteousness" (Ephesians 6:14; D&C 27:16). But just in case you think that means you need to muster up a greater level of righteousness, let me stop you right there. We already said that each piece of armor represents a part of Jesus's nature that He's going to share with us—*His* righteousness, not our own. What we're doing when we strap on this particular breastplate is covering ourselves in our Prince's perfect goodness. We're participating in the Great Exchange, just like we talked about in an earlier scene.

You may be wondering why your good works won't be enough to protect you while in battle. After all, you're probably doing a ton of tithe-paying, church-going, scripture-reading, and commandment-keeping, so shouldn't that count as some pretty sound armor? Unfortunately, this particular fight just doesn't work that way. Let me show you a few verses from the New Testament to explain why that's the case.

First, in Galatians 3, Paul says, "For as many as are of the works of the law are under the curse: for it is written, *Cursed* is every one that continueth not in *all* things which are written in the book of the law to do them" (Galatians 3:10; emphasis added).

Basically, he's saying that when it comes to keeping the law, the Lord's standard is perfection or nothing. We must do *all* things written in God's law or we're cursed. Period. And James adds this frightening little tidbit: "Whosoever shall keep the whole law, and yet offend in one point, *he is guilty of all*" (James 2:10; emphasis added). Yikes. Break even one commandment and it's the same as if you've broken them all. Put these two scriptures together and we can see where that leaves our little homemade breastplate of good works.

Whenever we rely on our own righteous works to form a breastplate, the truth is that we'll always (always!) end up falling short. No matter how hard we try, we can never live God's law *perfectly* like Paul and James just said to. It's the reason Paul points out, "There is none righteous, no, not one," for "all have sinned, and come short of the glory of God" (Romans 3:10, 23). We may think we've forged thick enough steel through the many good works we've done, but under the surface, our failures and shortcomings will continue to cause huge holes and weak places, rendering our homemade breastplate useless. On our own, our works will never be enough to cover us and protect us from our devious enemy.

However, us relying on the breastplate of our Prince's righteousness will have an entirely different outcome. His perfect goodness, perfect sinlessness, and perfect obedience have forged a breastplate stronger than the thickest steel you can even imagine. And the amazing news is, when we strap on this powerful breastplate—meaning we participate in the Great Exchange and receive Christ's righteousness as our own—we no longer have to gauge our worthiness by our individual performance. Clothed in this mighty breastplate, we can boldly say, "It doesn't matter who I was in the past. I'm now covered by my Savior's perfect righteousness, and I'm 'relying wholly upon the merits of him who is mighty to save'" (2 Nephi 31:19).

I'd even dare suggest that the breastplate of righteousness has magical properties that protect us in ways we've never before experienced. For starters, think about where the breastplate sits. It's placed directly over your *heart*, is it not? And your heart is the seat of your most sensitive feelings and emotions. So let's look at what happens to your heart when you tried to rely on your own righteousness (or your own homemade armor) for protection. The minute you sin, fail, or falter, the enemy jumps at the chance to ridicule you, mock you, and discourage you by whispering, "You're a failure. You'll never be good enough. You can't do anything right." And what happens to your heart in that moment? Aren't you flooded with feelings of inadequacy, worthlessness, and despair? Don't you feel hopeless, like you'll never be able to measure up to the Lord's seemingly unattainable standard? All that pain and misery just shows how easy it is for the enemy to slice straight through your homemade armor and wound the tender feelings of your heart.

Now here's where the magic of our Prince's breastplate comes in. Because our Savior knows we're going to fail and fall short, He's provided the breastplate of *His* righteousness to cover all the vulnerable parts our heart. As Paul says, "By the obedience of one shall many be made righteous" (Romans 5:19). And one of the best parts about this gift is that we no longer have to struggle with painful feelings of inadequacy, worthlessness, or despair.

If you doubt you can ever overcome your feelings of worthlessness and inadequacy, answer me this: How can you ever get discouraged when your heart is clothed in Jesus Christ's glorious goodness? How can you ever feel inadequate when you know you no longer have to try to be righteous on your own? How can you feel like a failure when you know your Prince is there to sustain you, strengthen you, and forgive your every single sin and mistake? There really is nothing like the breastplate to keep your heart from falling into the depths of depression, hopelessness, or despair.

Okay, after strapping on the belt of truth and the breastplate of righteousness, what are we told to do next? It's time to have our "feet shod with the preparation of the gospel of peace" (Ephesians 6:15; D&C 27:16). Why make such a fuss over the feet of a warrior? Well, imagine what would happen if a soldier put on a full suit of armor then ran out to fight without any boots on. He wouldn't last long, would he? It reminds me of the great Achilles in Greek mythology. As a baby, Achilles's mother dipped him in the magical River Styx to protect him from death. But because she held him by the heel, that part of his body was unprotected, which left him with one small area of weakness. While that tiny spot may not have seemed like much of a threat, it was a wound to his heel that eventually took Achilles's life. It just goes to show that our enemy is aware of even our smallest weaknesses, so we need to make sure we're completely covered with Christ's enabling power. In order to conquer the villain, even our feet must be covered, protected, and anchored securely on solid ground.

When Paul was writing about the armor of God, I like to think he was imagining a Roman soldier in all his splendor. A Roman warrior's shoes were definitely a creative part of his battle uniform. Known as *caligae*, these special boots actually had "iron hobnails . . . hammered into the soles to provide . . . reinforcement and traction."[3] Can you imagine how firmly your feet would be anchored to the ground if you had nails sticking out of the bottom? That's the image I want you to remember as we talk about the shoes you'll be wearing as part of the armor of God.

Notice also that Paul didn't say we should have our feet shod with the gospel of peace, but with the *preparation* of that gospel. The Greek word for preparation in that phrase is *hetoimasia*, which actually means "foundation" or "firm footing."[4] So the question is, how does the gospel of Jesus Christ give our feet firm footing to stand on? How does our Savior anchor us in battle as firmly as a pair of Roman hobnailed boots?

I believe that, just like it says in both accounts, our firm footing can be found in the "gospel of *peace*." But we're not talking about some sort of general peace here. No, we're talking about the peace you feel when you finally know you're right with your Father in Heaven—when, because of your Savior's Atonement, you're no longer an "enemy to God" (Mosiah 3:19), and when you're no longer "shut out" (2 Nephi 9:9), "endlessly lost" (Mosiah 16:4), or "cut off from [your Father's] presence" (Alma 42:9). That knowledge brings a powerful kind of peace that's incredibly hard to describe. It's the rock solid peace that comes from knowing your Prince is on your side and He's promised to never ever leave you, fail you, or forsake you (see Joshua 1:5 and Hebrews 13:5).

Just like hobnailed boots, these precious shoes anchor us in the knowledge that Jesus Christ is our "rock" and our "salvation" (Psalm 62:6). He is our "strength" and our "song" (2 Nephi 22:2). Even more important, we're anchored in the fact that "neither death, nor life, nor angels, nor principalities, nor powers, nor things present, nor things to come, nor height, nor depth, nor any other creature, shall be able to separate us from the love of God, which is in Christ Jesus our Lord" (Romans 8:38–39). Just like the caligae, these boots will never slip, slide, or give way while in the heat of battle.

In the end, I think the shoes are summed up perfectly in this one beautiful phrase: "*He* is our peace" (Ephesians 2:14; emphasis added). Notice, even though our blessed Savior can definitely *give us* His peace (John 14:27), in an even greater way, He Himself *is* our peace. For with Him by our side, we know we can win the battle against the enemy. With Him by our side, all our anxiety and fear will be swallowed up in His love. With Him by our side, we really can be transformed back into celestial princesses. There's not more solid ground we can stand on than that. Only Christ can "guide our feet into the way of peace" and keep us firmly anchored on the rock of His solid foundation (Luke 1:79).

All right, princess warrior, are you ready to move on to the next piece of armor? If you remember, it's called the "helmet of salvation" (Ephesians 6:17; D&C 27:18). To show you why we need it, let me share a little story with you. One Sunday, I was teaching a lesson to our ward Young Women, and the girls and I were talking about how awkward it would be if other people could read our minds. My daughter suggested, "What if we had a big thought bubble over our heads and everyone around us could see every little thing we're thinking?" The idea disturbed most of us because of all the embarrassing and sinful things that pass through our minds on a daily basis. One Beehive even moaned that people would think she was crazy if they could see everything she was thinking. I'm guessing you feel the same way the girls and I did. Like us, I'm sure you can think of plenty of junk that's hidden inside your head.

Why are our minds so messed up, anyway? Why do we think so many impure, rebellious, and sinful thoughts? The answer is simple: because we've been living in the dragon's lair. It doesn't take long in that dreary environment for all kinds of lies, insecurities, and fears to work their way into our minds. So we need our Prince's help to sort it all out. And that's where the helmet of salvation comes in. Notice where this piece of armor sits: right on top of our head.

The word *salvation* means "deliverance from the power and effects of sin."[5] By providing this strong covering for our heads, our Prince is offering to protect our minds from the many side effects of sin. Remember, He "know[s] the things that come into [our] mind, every one of them" (Ezekiel 11:5). He knows our minds have been "darkened" (D&C 10:2) and "hardened in pride" (Daniel 5:20) while we've lived as a dragon. He knows we've suffered from "blindness of mind" (Ether 4:15) and "vanity of . . . mind" (Ephesians 4:17), and that we become "wearied and faint in [our] minds" from time to time (Hebrews 12:3). Thankfully, through His grace, we can actually be "transformed by the renewing of [our] mind" (Romans 12:2).

It's just like the scripture we quoted earlier: "God hath not given us the spirit of fear; but of power, and of love, and of a *sound mind*" (2 Timothy 1:7; emphasis added). A sound mind is a mind that is healthy, untroubled, and free from weakness or error. Wouldn't you love to have a mind like that? It really is possible, but only if you'll let your Prince mess up your hair and place the helmet of salvation firmly on your pretty little head. There's more to this particular covering in battle, but for now, let's move on to another really cool piece of the armor of light.

Up next we have the bold and mighty "sword of the Spirit" (Ephesians 6:17). Notice that it's not a piece of defensive armor but an offensive weapon we can use to strike down our enemy. However, this particular sword can be a little tricky to understand because it's described differently in the two passages of scripture. For instance, Paul tells us in Ephesians that we must take the "sword of the Spirit, which is the word of God" (Ephesians 6:17). But then Doctrine and Covenants says we must take "the sword

of my Spirit, which I will pour out upon you, and my word which I reveal unto you" (D&C 27:18). So does the sword of the Spirit represent the word of God like Paul says, or are they two separate things like it seems to say in Doctrine and Covenants? We can turn to some other verses of scripture to help us better understand this powerful and influential weapon.

For starters, in the Doctrine and Covenants Our prince describes His word five different times as "sharper than a two-edged sword" (D&C 6:2; 11:2; 12:2; 14:2; and 33:1). And Paul portrays it the same way in the book of Hebrews:

> For the word of God is quick, and powerful, and sharper than any twoedged sword, piercing even to the dividing asunder of soul and spirit, and of the joints and marrow, and is a discerner of the thoughts and intents of the heart. (Hebrews 4:12)

So according to these verses, Christ's word has the power of not just of a regular sword but a *two-edged* sword that can cut both ways and "[divide] asunder" the "soul and spirit." But how can a bunch of little black letters on a thin little page have that kind of power? We'll find a clue in the scripture we just read in Hebrews. Look at it again and note how Paul described the word of God as "quick."[6] Don't you think that's an odd term for the Apostle to use? Just think of all the other adjectives he could have chosen—words like *good, pure, holy, righteous,* or even *faithful.* Why call our Prince's word "quick"? The answer is hidden in the Greek word Paul used for *quick* in Hebrews 4:12: *zao.* Surprisingly, it doesn't mean speedy, fast, or even brisk. No, this special word actually means "alive" or "living."[7]

With that in mind, now listen to the way our Prince describes the scriptures in the Doctrine and Covenants (and make sure to watch for the word *quick* in this verse as well): "The Book of Mormon and the holy scriptures are given of me for your instruction; *and the power of my Spirit quickeneth all things*" (D&C 33:16; emphasis added). Now things are finally coming together. Here we learn the Spirit is what "quickens" the word of God, or brings the Prince's word to life. So we're going to view the sword as the

word of God when it's connected with the life-giving power of the Spirit.

I'm sure you can see it isn't any ordinary sword. Perhaps you could picture it in your mind just like King Arthur's legendary Excalibur. It's a weapon that holds the power to "divide asunder all the cunning and the snares and the wiles of the devil, and lead the man of Christ in a strait and narrow course across that everlasting gulf of misery which is prepared to engulf the wicked" (Helaman 3:29). You've probably seen a swordfight in movies, so you know that a sword like this isn't an easy weapon to use. It takes a great deal of training and practice to learn how to handle it correctly. For this reason, we're going to take a lot of time in the next chapter learning how to use this weapon in such a way that it strikes fear in the heart of our enemy. But while we're learning to use that sword, we'll need the last piece of armor: the incomparable shield of faith.

I hope you're ready to use your imagination again, because this isn't one of those small circular shields like Captain America carries. Even though that kind of shield can be helpful in battle, we're going to need something much bigger for the challenge we've got ahead. Paul understood this, so he chose the Greek word *thureos*, which is a "large and oblong [shield], protecting every part of the soldier."[8] It's the type of shield a soldier could dig into the ground and put his entire body behind. We're talking about complete and total protection here—a barrier that can block out every possible assault the enemy can throw our way.

The reason I left the shield of faith for last is because it really does tie all the other pieces of armor together. You see, the belt of truth can make you as devoted and steadfast as an oak, but if you don't *believe* it can do what your Prince says it will, the band will fall right off your waist. The breastplate of Christ's righteousness can cover all your weaknesses and insecurities, but if you don't *believe* it can do what your Prince says it will, the enemy's arrows will pierce your heart. The helmet of salvation can guard your mind against the villain's malicious lies, but if you don't *believe* it can do what your Prince says it will, your thoughts will be vulnerable to all kinds of mental attacks. The shoes of peace can provide

the comfort of knowing you're accepted of God, but if you don't *believe* they can do what your Prince says they will, you'll be left barefoot in the middle of the fray. Simply put, every piece of armor works according to your faith. Your faith in Jesus Christ really does form a shield around you to guard you against the many attacks of the adversary.

But that's not all. We need to take it one step further because it's not enough just to believe something is true. You also have to believe everything we just talked about is true *for you personally*. No matter what you've done, no matter how badly you've messed up, you have to believe your Hero really can make you into a princess warrior. In fact, if this scene doesn't become personal, you'll just end up lying wounded in the corner while others around you rise up to fight.

I'd like to end our discussion on the armor of light right back where we began. As you prepare yourself to follow your Prince into battle, please don't forget that Jesus Christ Himself is your armor of light. *He* is your belt. *He* is your breastplate. *He* is your helmet. *He* is your solid foundation. *He* is your sword. And *He* is your shield. Suited up in this precious armor, you receive His commitment to buoy you up, His righteousness to remove your guilt and shame, His peace to wipe away your fear, His faith to fight off any doubt, His helmet to protect your mind, and His sword to strike down all the cunning attacks of the enemy. Your job is simply to believe that it will be enough to help you conquer the villain.

Okay, we've finally reached the point where it all comes together. Now that your faith has truly become personal—meaning Jesus Christ truly has become your personal Savior, and you believe deep down that His truth, righteousness, peace, salvation, and Spirit are available for *you*—then the armor of light will lock tightly into place. It will feel so empowering, you'll wonder how you ever tried to battle the enemy without it. With this ironclad protection fit snugly around you, it's finally time to jump into the next scene. And it's full of intense, nonstop action. Are you ready to go head to head with the evil villain and his army of minions?

Brace yourself, because this scene has the potential to be quite a dramatic fight.

For Additional Study

When it comes to the sword or the word of God, we talked a lot about how it can be "quick," but we didn't spend as much time studying how it can be "powerful." When Paul described the word of God this way, he used the Greek word *energes*, which means "active."[9] (Now you can see where we got the English word *energy*!). To understand how the sword can be "powerful" or "active" in our lives, read Alma 5:13 and 31:5. Look at the influence of the "word" in each verse and what it was able to accomplish.

In 1 Thessalonians, Paul says we should put on "for an helmet, the *hope* of salvation" (1 Thessalonians 5:8; emphasis added). I believe the Apostle added *hope* to this piece of armor because it's an incredibly powerful defense against the enemy. As President Dieter F. Uchtdorf reminds us,

> Hope is . . . the abiding trust that the Lord will fulfill His promise to us. It is confidence that if we live according to God's laws and the words of His prophets now, we will receive desired blessings in the future. It is believing and expecting that our prayers will be answered. It is manifest in confidence, optimism, enthusiasm, and patient perseverance. . . . Hope sustains us through despair. Hope teaches that there is reason to rejoice even when all seems dark around us.[10]

Take some time to study scriptures on hope in the Topical Guide. Journal what you learn about this beautiful and comforting word. Like President Uchtdorf said, hope really can give you all the optimism, enthusiasm, and perseverance you could possibly need.

One final point about the helmet of salvation. You need to know that your media choices will have a huge influence on your ability to keep this helmet in place, especially music. Because music lyrics tend to get stuck in your head, the songs you listen to will have a powerful influence on your inner thoughts and beliefs. Immersing yourself in worldly music will allow the villain's deceitful ideas to crowd out your Prince's truth. So take some time to evaluate how you can fill your environment with as much uplifting music as possible. And I'm not just talking about the Mormon Tabernacle Choir and other wonderful LDS artists. There's a ton of awesome Christian music out there. Just look up MercyMe, Casting Crowns, Matthew West, Big Daddy Weave, or Mandisa and you'll see what I mean. Or you can check out Christian radio on Pandora or get the app for klove.com. You'll find so many amazing and uplifting artists, you'll never want to listen to worldly music ever again!

AN EPIC BATTLE

I N THE MOVIES, have you ever noticed how the big battle scenes often start with a bird's-eye view of the two armies on the battlefield? I love how the camera takes extra time panning over the enemy army. As the viewer takes in the gruesome soldiers, razor-sharp weapons, and fierce-looking animals, feelings of tension build to quite a fevered pitch. This technique works because it shows the audience what a dangerous enemy the heroes are up against, and it also makes the victory that much more sweet in the end. For this reason, we're going to start our battle scene with the same panoramic view. I too want you to know exactly what you're facing as you go into battle against the evil villain and his menacing band of minions.

By now you know enough about your enemy to imagine him in all of his nastiness and deceitfulness. And don't forget to picture the massive army of angels by his side, ready to do all they can to build his kingdom. Paul was right when he said, "We wrestle not against flesh and blood, but against principalities, against powers, against the rulers of the darkness of this world" (Ephesians 6:12). We're about to wage war against an invisible but incredibly daunting opponent. Nevertheless, this is a fight we need to win. It's the only way we can escape life in the dragon's lair once and for all.

I must warn you that as soon as Satan realizes you're trying to break free from his clutches, he's going to come at you with every weapon in his arsenal. You've been his prisoner for a long time, and he's not going to give you up without a fight. But just because he can't use a real sword to draw your blood or a real bomb to blow you up, don't think he doesn't have any weapons. He's actually an expert at using what the scriptures call his "fiery darts" (Ephesians 6:16). It's a good description because these flaming arrows can pierce you and they can burn. If the poison from one of his darts gets inside you, it can paralyze you and take you right out of the fight.

Watch yourself, because in this particular scene, Satan is going to do everything he can to deceive you (D&C 50:3), overpower your testimony (D&C 10:33), and turn your heart from the truth (D&C 78:10). He'll try to cause all kinds of contention (3 Nephi 11:29), put false ideas in your heart (1 Timothy 4:1; D&C 10:10), and even possess you personally or through the use of his sneaky little sidekicks (Matthew 8:16). In short, he'll do everything he can to make you afraid, make you doubt, or make you sin. He'll try to bully you, discourage you, or leave you feeling like you're all alone. He'll lie to you about your life, your family, your beliefs, your future, and your salvation. And he'll laugh hardest of all if he can get you to lose faith in your Prince.

That's not even the worst of it. Satan may instead turn the tables and try to flatter you into thinking he doesn't even exist (2 Nephi 28:22). Or he'll pacify you into believing you don't need to repent or there's nothing wrong with the way the world is telling you to live (2 Nephi 28:21). The Bible Dictionary says that "one of [his] major techniques . . . is to cause [you] to think [you] are following God's ways, when in reality [you] are deceived [into following] other paths."[1] I tell you these things because I don't want you to underestimate the power of your enemy. Remember, at this moment you are not yet on neutral ground. Through your natural man, you're still the prisoner of an extremely vile and manipulative enemy—and he wants to keep it that way.

The odd thing about this scene is that we've already spent a great deal of time on this battlefield, only we haven't fared that well in the past. Though we probably mustered up enough strength to fend off the enemy here and there, we've still succumbed to his advances, listened to his lies, and acted on his temptations. Knocked to the ground again and again, we've struggled to find a way to conquer the villain once and for all. We desperately wanted to win this fight and rid ourselves of our personal dragon scales— we just haven't known how to do it.

Now we stand here, outfitted in our Prince's armor of light. While we may think we're finally ready to triumph on the battle-field, let me remind you that just because you're wearing the right gear doesn't mean you'll immediately conquer the adversary. This fight will be a fierce one, and you still need one more thing to suc-ceed. What in the world could we add to our heavy armor, thick shield, and two-edged sword? It's our Prince's *power*, of course, or his strengthening, enabling *grace*. And we don't just need a little of it—we need Christ's grace to fill us from the top of our head down to the tips of our little toes.

A perfect example of what can happen in battle when we're filled with our Prince's grace is found in the movie *Percy Jackson and the Olympians: The Lightning Thief*. In this particular scene, Percy had recently arrived at Camp Half-Blood, where he learned that his real father was Poseidon, the god of the sea. Immediately the young man's warrior training began, and he soon found him self in a serious game of capture the flag. Percy did everything he knew how to win, but just as he was about to grab the flag in victory, he came face to face with Annabeth, the daughter of the goddess Athena. Annabeth was skilled with the sword, and despite Percy's best efforts, the young woman struck him down in only a matter of minutes.

Now for my favorite part of all. As Percy lay on the ground wounded and bleeding, he suddenly heard his father's voice whis-per, "Go to the water. The water will give you power." In faith, Percy crawled to the bank and dipped his hand carefully into the edge of the stream. Instantly, his father's power began to travel up his hand and throughout his entire body, filling him with strength and healing him of all his wounds. Percy rose up to fight with such courage and boldness, he bested not only Annabeth but her entire team of cohorts.[2] It was truly an inspiring triumph, and one that has a great deal to do with this part of our princess story.

Just like Percy, we too are children of a God. But that hasn't stopped our enemy from defeating us time and time again with all different types of sin and temptation. In true Annabeth fashion, Satan comes at us with all his fiery darts and often levels us in a matter of minutes, only our wounds aren't physical like Percy's— they cut deep into the recesses of our minds and hearts.

Thankfully, we've discovered an amazing Rescuer, who's empowered us for battle. He's given us the armor of light, the sword of the Spirit, and the shield of faith, but it won't be enough unless we do the same thing Percy did—"go to the water" to be filled with Christ's enabling grace. Why is our Prince's power so important? Let me read you a few verses from Doctrine and Covenants 105, and I think you'll finally understand what's taking place on this particular battlefield and why we can't succeed unless we truly "abound in [our Savior's] grace" (2 Corinthians 8:7).

Doctrine and Covenants 105 is a revelation given in 1834 to an army of brethren called Zion's Camp, and it talks quite a bit about how to deal with battles and war. Listen to this haunting verse that applies to the current scene of our story:

> Behold, I have commanded my servant Joseph Smith, Jun., to say unto the strength of my house, even my warriors, my young men, and middle-aged, to gather together for the redemption of my people, and throw down the towers of mine enemies, and scatter their watchmen; *but the strength of mine house have not hearkened unto my words.* (D&C 105:16–17)

I know we may have failed to hearken to our Prince in the past, but hopefully we've now learned to follow His every word with exactness. However, in this section, the Lord points out something else that must happen for us to throw down the enemy's towers and scatter his watchmen. He says, "But first let my army become very great, and let it be sanctified before me, that it may become fair as the sun, and clear as the moon, and that her banners may be terrible unto all nations" (D&C 105:31).

Notice that before we can be victorious, we must first be *sanctified*, meaning we must be baptized by fire and received a remission of our sins. Once that happens, we really will be "more than

conquerors through him that loved us" (Romans 8:37). Like the Lord said, we'll be "fair" as the sun, "clear" as the moon, and "terrible as an army with banners" (see D&C 5:14; 109:73).

Just for clarity's sake, I want to look at the definitions of *fair*, *clear*, and *terrible* so we can paint a mental picture of exactly what our Prince is talking about. To be *fair as the sun* means our hearts are bright, sunny, and free from any storms or clouds.[3] The word *clear* also refers to being "free from darkness [or] obscurity."[4] But I think *terrible* is the coolest one of all: "formidably great," or one that excites "terror, awe, or great fear" in all who may be looking on.[5] Put those words together and we learn that a princess warrior's heart must be free of darkness and so full of strength and light that she inspires wonder and awe in all those who encounter her.

And that right there is the reason we need our Prince's grace. He doesn't just share it with us to make us strong and powerful. He shares it with us *so we can be sanctified*, so our dragon skin can be removed once and for all, so we can "chase darkness from among [us]" (D&C 50:25). Only Christ holds the power to remove Satan's influence completely from our lives. Only He can enable us to put off our natural man and once again become not only a royal princess but a formidable and bold princess warrior.

I hope you're ready, because once you're "armed with . . . the power of God in great glory" (1 Nephi 14:14), you can finally go into battle with all the courage, strength, and wisdom you could possibly need. Please note that this kind of combat won't play out on an enormous field filled with soldiers, tanks, and artillery, but in the hidden places of your mind and heart. It's a battle that perhaps only you will know about, but it's a crucial battle nonetheless. Paul described this fight to cleanse our minds and sanctify our hearts with these inspiring words:

> For though we walk in the flesh, we do not war after the flesh: (for the weapons of our warfare are not carnal, but mighty through God to the pulling down of strong holds;) casting down imaginations, and every high thing that exalteth itself against the knowledge of God, and bringing into captivity every thought to the obedience of Christ. (2 Corinthians 10:3–5)

According to Paul, to be sanctified we must strike down any "imaginations" in our minds that exalt themselves above the knowledge of our Prince. These are the sinful weeds we've been talking about all along—the thoughts planted in our minds by the villain and his trusty sidekicks. In order to "[bring] into captivity every thought to the obedience of Christ," we must cast out the lies quietly living inside us, and also strike down any new lies the enemy and his helpers try to get us to believe.

If you're wondering how you'll know when a fiery dart is approaching, I'll give you a clue. If you "watch yourselves, and your thoughts, and your words, and your deeds" (Mosiah 4:30), you'll notice almost immediately if something isn't right. For instance, if you start to feel discouraged or depressed, if you experience a strong pull toward the things of the world, or if a spirit of envy, greed, or contention threatens to overwhelm you—you can know without a doubt that you're under attack. That's the moment you need to rely on your Prince and your armor with absolutely everything you have.

If the villain is tempting you to lay aside your scriptures in favor of your phone, picture the belt of truth wrapped tightly around your core, making you as solid and steadfast as an oak. If he's trying to get you to turn to worldly things for comfort or escape, imagine those fiery darts clattering to the floor the minute they strike your impenetrable helmet. If he's attempting to shame you for all of your past faults and failures, visualize the breastplate of your Prince's perfect righteousness shielding all your sins from the view of your Father in Heaven. Only as you make the armor of God a real thing in your life will each piece be able to guard you from the many wiles of the adversary.

However, your most effective defense will be your offense—or the "quick and powerful" sword of the Spirit (D&C 11:2). To show you how this mighty sword works in battle, let's review some of the most common lies the adversary likes to fire our way. See if any of these fiery darts have planted their poison deep inside the thoughts of your head.

LIE: I can't do anything right.

LIE: God doesn't answer my prayers.

LIE: My body will never be beautiful or attractive.

LIE: I have no one to turn to.

LIE: My sins are too hard to overcome.

LIE: I don't feel like my Savior really loves me.

Have any of these arrows ever wounded you or knocked you off your feet? If so, now you know exactly how to deal with them. In addition to relying on your armor to keep these falsehoods from penetrating your heart and mind, you can also strike back with the sword, or the Spirit-infused word of your Prince that comes to you in moments of temptation. Here's an example of how the battle may unfold.

Let's say you're struggling with a personal weakness, and Satan whispers his first little lie into your thoughts: *You can't do anything right.* Immediately, you counter with the word of God by pondering the scripture "I can do all things through Christ which strengtheneth me" (Philippians 4:13). Later that day, something you prayed about seems to fall through, and the enemy quietly launches his next lie: *God never answers your prayers.* Quickly, you draw the sword and hit him back with the verse "In the day of my trouble I will call upon [God]: for [He] wilt answer me" (Psalm 86:7). When you're getting ready for bed, you catch a glimpse of yourself in the mirror, and the next lie comes sailing through the air: *You're fat and ugly. Who would ever love someone who looks like you?* By now you don't even flinch. Rather than giving in to that thought, you meet the attack with boldness by repeating, "I am fearfully and wonderfully made" (Psalm 139:14) and, "In the image of [God's] own body . . . [am I] created" (Moses 6:9).

On and on it goes. Every time the enemy sends his deceitful darts your way, you use your Prince's word as a sword to strike them down. (Of course, you have to spend lots of time in the scriptures so you'll be able to wield the sword with accuracy.) Using the standard works and the words of the prophets and apostles is an incredibly powerful way to deflect the fiery darts of the enemy.

In the Book of Mormon, many different prophets used the word of God as a weapon when they battled Satan's sidekicks. Jacob did that with Sherem (Jacob 7), Alma used it against Korihor (Alma 30), and it also worked for Amulek when he faced Zeezrom

(Alma 11). Believe it or not, even the Lord Himself relied on this strategy during his earthly ministry. When the enemy confronted Jesus while He was in the wilderness, He answered every temptation the devil threw at Him by quoting verses from the Old Testament.

When Satan tempted Him to turn stones into bread, the Lord boldly replied, "*It is written*, Man shall not live by bread alone, but by every word that proceedeth out of the mouth of God" (Matthew 4:4; emphasis added). When the enemy encouraged Him to display His power in a self-promoting way, Christ answered, "*It is written again*, Thou shalt not tempt the Lord thy God" (Matthew 4:7; emphasis added). Finally, when Lucifer offered to give Jesus all the kingdoms of the earth, our Prince once more relied on the word as a sword by saying, "Get thee hence, Satan: *for it is written*, Thou shalt worship the Lord thy God, and him only shalt thou serve" (Matthew 4:10; emphasis added). And you must use the same strategy every time the enemy's darts come whooshing through the air. Whether it's one of your peers tempting you to do something or one of Satan's henchmen trying to convince you to believe devious little lies, you must meet that assault with the sword of the Spirit, or the word of God that's been so generously provided by your Prince.

One of the trickiest things about this battle is that some of the enemy's fiery darts are already lodged deep inside your heart. We talked earlier about how the villain has worked hard over the years to plant his lies inside you without you even realizing it. As we've gone through this story, I hope you discovered many of those hidden falsehoods and wrote them down in your journal. If you have, it's now time to rip those lies right out of your mind and heart.

For example, if you've believed the lie that no one is there for you, you can shred that falsehood by memorizing your Prince's promise: "I am with you to bless you and deliver you forever" (D&C 108:8). If you've believed the lie that you're too weak to overcome your sins, you can slice it to pieces by pondering your Savior's words: "My grace is sufficient for all men that humble themselves before me; for . . . I [will] make weak things become strong unto them" (Ether 12:27). If you believed the lie that your Redeemer doesn't know or care about you personally, you can pull out that fiery dart by reviewing your Hero's blessed assurance: "As the Father hath loved me, so have I loved you: continue ye in my love" (John 15:9). Every time you use the Lord's word as a sword, you're confronting the villain head on and showing him that his lies aren't going to work on you anymore.

It's exactly what Rapunzel did when she confronted Gothel at the end of the movie *Tangled*. Once she learned the truth of who she really was, Rapunzel realized she didn't have to play the evil woman's game any longer. I love it when Rapunzel boldly tells Gothel, "You were wrong about the world, and you were wrong about me." It's a powerful moment that changed Rapunzel's life forever. Though the battle wasn't necessarily over, Gothel could no longer use her lies to control and manipulate the vulnerable princess.

Just like with Rapunzel, the villain has told you things about yourself and about the world that are flat-out wrong. But now you have your Prince's word to support and sustain you, and you can stand your ground with the same boldness and firmness Rapunzel showed against her enemy. However, in order for this sword to truly be effective, you can't just review the Prince's truth and leave it at that. You must also hold up the shield of faith and show that you *believe* every single word your Savior is telling you. I'll admit it's sometimes easier said than done, especially in the beginning stages of the battle.

Think about the inner conflict Rapunzel experienced when she first stepped outside the tower. The lie that Gothel was her mother and she must be obedient to her wishes still wielded a great deal of power over the princess's heart. As a result, she battled feelings of fear and guilt as soon as she moved outside the established boundary. You know the scene I'm talking about: one minute Rapunzel was gleefully shouting about how good it felt to be free, and the next minute she was convinced she needed to go back. Back and forth she went between her urge to break free and the guilt she felt for going against Gothel's wishes. She really was at war with herself, just like Eugene said. Because Rapunzel still believed the lies, she was torn between the new world she was experiencing and the old one that felt so comfortable. Rapunzel had accepted Gothel's falsehoods for so long that it took some time for her to get used to living without them.

So please don't panic if the same thing happens to you when you begin rooting out the lies that have been hiding deep inside your mind and heart. Often the enemy's lies have attached themselves so strongly to your thoughts and feelings, it can be hard to believe your Prince when He begins to tell you the truth. For instance, if the Lord whispers the truth that you are loved and cherished, you may struggle to believe His words because you still *feel* alone and unloved. However, you've got to remember that your feelings have been manipulated by the enemy, so you can't always rely on them to determine what's true. What you *can* trust is your Prince's word, engraved on the pages of scripture and coming to you through prophets, apostles, and even the voice of your Hero Himself.

If your Savior gently reminds you that He loves you and will be with you, you must trust He's telling the truth—even if you don't *feel* it at first. I promise, if you'll continue to keep your eyes and ears fastened on your Prince, His word will eventually become real for you and you'll be able to cast out the lies you've believed about yourself, about others, and about the world. Just like Christ promised, "ye shall know the truth, and the truth shall make you free" (John 8:32).

There's also another way you can end up at war with yourself, and it's over the difficult issue of self-control. Satan loves to whisper again and again that you'll never have enough self-control to win the fight against sin. It can be tempting to believe this lie because it often feels like he's telling the truth. In the past, you really *have* committed the same old sins over and over, so it's easy to accept the lie that you'll never be able to stop yourself from doing those things at some point in the future. So what will keep you from succumbing to depression and self-pity when the villain reminds you of all your failures? What will keep you from hanging your head and thinking, *It really is true—I don't have any self-control. I'll never be able to stop committing this or that particular sin?*

Believe it or not, there *is* way to get all the self-control you could possibly need. And it will come as you reach out, grab the sword of the Spirit, and lift it boldly and confidently in the air. Here's the specific word of God that we'll use for this particular attack: "But the fruit of the Spirit is love, joy, peace, longsuffering, gentleness, goodness, faith, meekness, [and] temperance" (Galatians 5:22–23). See that word *temperance* at the end of the verse? Guess what it means in the original Greek language? *Self-control.*[6] In other words, this verse is telling us that temperance—the ability to restrain ourselves from sinful thoughts and actions—comes through the power of the Spirit. Only the Prince can endow us with all the self-control we need to stand against temptation.

This is wonderful news because the next time you face that same old sin, now you know how to fight back. Rather than trying to muster up more willpower or make promises to yourself that you know you won't keep, this time you can rely wholly on the power of your Prince. Like Percy at the water's edge, you can turn to Christ and soak up enough grace to give you a strong sense of temperance or self-control. This supernatural power will fill you, strengthen you, and fortify you in even the most difficult moments of temptation. As LDS author and leader Sheri Dew reminds us, "Because Jesus Christ atoned, his grace is available to us every minute of every hour of every day."[7]

In this battle scene, you really are doing exactly what Rapunzel did—you're fighting to cast out the lies you've believed in order to reveal the true princess hiding underneath that prickly dragon skin. To remove those dragon scales for good, a big part of this battle must include going back through your journal and letting your Prince help you work through each and every one of your individual sins. Be brave, and let Him shine His light on your family relationships, your relationships with your friends (both girls and guys), your feelings about your body, your hobbies and extracurricular activities, your challenges and trials, your leisure time, your Church service, and even your hopes and dreams. Satan has led you to believe his lies in many of these different areas, and it's time to destroy those falsehoods with the help of your Prince and the sword of the Spirit. As you open yourself to your Savior's magnificent "grace and truth" (2 Nephi 2:6), He will show you how to deal with every single issue, no matter how tough or painful it may be. He'll peel off your dragon scales one by one, and you'll slowly be transformed into the princess you were always meant to become.

For me, this part of the battle included dismantling my negative body image,[8] unraveling some unhealthy family dynamics I'd grown up with, and discarding some false gods I'd adopted to help me cope with my emotional pain. For a friend of mine, this part of the battle involved laying aside her controlling tendencies and learning to let go and let the Lord take the lead. For another friend, it included casting out the lies caused by childhood bullying—the lies that everyone hated her and would eventually leave her or abuse her. For yet another friend, it involved demolishing the lie that there were too many people in the world and the Lord could never know her personally. Though my friends and I all dealt with different issues, we each discovered that our Prince had enough power to peel off those awful dragon scales that were wrapped so firmly around our minds and hearts.

To put it another way, what we're doing in this battle is casting away the false self we created when we found ourselves stuck in the dragon's lair. Being a dragon hasn't been pleasant, so most of us have tried hard to hide our dark side from the rest of the world. To do this, we created a mask we could wear—a false self we could present to others to make it look like we had it all together. These are the counterfeit ways of living we talked about earlier, or the things we relied on to make ourselves feel more secure and successful.

Unfortunately, it can be extremely difficult to let go of our personal mask. In the past, we've trusted that mask to cover our pain, our disappointments, our faults, our brokenness, and our insecurities. We've worn it to avoid being shamed, hurt, judged, or rejected. We've put it on to convince others (and even ourselves) that we are strong, righteous, and perfect rather than flawed, weak, and mortal. We've used it to win the popularity of our peers or to make others think we're cool. But in the end, that mask hid our true selves from the world and kept us from becoming the people we are really meant to be.

If you want to know more about your own individual mask, you could ask yourself the following questions: Who have I been pretending to be when I'm around other people? Am I pretending that everything is okay when I know it's not? That I'm strong when I know I'm weak? That I'm happy when I'm actually in pain? That I've got it all together when I feel like a mess? That my family is perfect when we really have a lot of problems? That I don't need anyone's help when I'm really confused? That I have all the answers when deep down I feel hesitant and unsure? How you answer these questions matters, because each of these scenarios describe ways we use a masks to cope with and cover our dragon nature. And, royal princess, the time has come to rip off that covering once and for all.

If you'll lean in a little closer, I'll whisper the real reason you need to throw away that deceptive covering: Your Prince has always been able to see what's behind it anyway. He knows who you really are, and He wants more than anything to unveil that beautiful person in all her uniqueness and splendor. He longs for you to know you don't have to masquerade for one moment longer. In truth, *He* is all the covering you could ever need.

Remember, you can't grip the sword of the Spirit or the shield of faith if you're busy holding up a mask. In fact, you may have noticed that the armor of God doesn't have any kind of facial covering at all. I believe that's because a real royal princess isn't afraid to show her true self to the outside world, the self that's been purified and transformed by the Lord Jesus Christ. It's why Christ gave His life for you in the first place—to save you and redeem you so you no longer have to hide behind a façade. What greater love could your Hero offer you than that?

Drenched in His deeply satisfying affection, I know you'll find the courage to throw away your personal mask for good. Let the Lord cleanse you, purify you, and save you from all the terrible years in the dragon's lair. Let Him peel off your dragon scales of perfectionism or your desperate need to win others' approval. Let Him heal your deep-seated fears or the scars you've borne from a painful past. Let Him shine His sun-soaked grace over all your wounds, failures, mistakes, and sins. Once He does, you really will be fair as the sun, clear as the moon, and terrible as an army with banners.

At this point, you may be wondering how you'll know when the battle is finally over. How can you tell that you've been baptized by fire and received a remission of your sins? It's simple, really. You'll know your Prince has changed you when you begin living each day differently. Suddenly, the insecurity and fear that used to plague you are no longer problems. That person who used to push your buttons doesn't irritate you like they used to. You find you've lost your appetite for worldly trends, and you enjoy spiritual things you previously found boring. Best of all, when you face those same temptations that used to nail you again and again, you strike down that personal assault with ease. In that moment, you'll know that you've been dramatically changed by an incredibly loving and powerful Savior.

In short, you'll know the battle is coming to an end when you begin thinking, speaking, and acting in a whole new way. No, you won't be completely sinless, but you'll no longer be stuck in the same sinful patterns, obsessions, and addictions that haunted you so often in the past. Instead, you'll feel radiant, vibrant, and filled with your Prince's heavenly light. When that moment comes, you'll be able to say with Alma, "I have repented of my sins, and have been redeemed of the Lord; behold I am born of the Spirit" (Mosiah 27:24). At last, you'll be transformed into a beautiful, grace-filled princess. Though you'll definitely keep your armor on for the rest of your life, now you'll know how to conquer the villain, so the most difficult part of the battle will finally be won.

I want you to picture with me the end of this scene where you'll walk out of the dragon's lair with your hand held tightly in that of your Prince. Where will you live now that you're no longer stuck in that dreary cavern? Just like any good princess story, the privilege is now yours to join your Hero in His shining and glorious kingdom. It's a world overflowing with peace, hope, joy, goodness, and love. Trust me when I tell you that life in your Redeemer's world will be far beyond anything you've ever experienced. Join me in the next scene as we explore what life will be like in our Prince's magical and wondrous new land.

For Additional Study

I hope it became obvious in this scene how important it is to work on memorizing different verses of scripture. It's not so we can boast about how many verses we know or so we can earn an award in seminary. We do it so the truths are readily available in our minds to strike down the enemy. I love how Elder Richard G. Scott describes this crucial practice (If I were you, I'd read his whole talk "The Power of Scripture." It's awesome!):

> Great power can come from memorizing scriptures. To memorize a scripture is to forge a new friendship. It is like discovering a new individual who can help in time of need, give inspiration and comfort, and be a source of motivation for needed change.[9]

My favorite way to memorize the scriptures is to write down the verses I'm working on in a 3 x 5 spiral notebook. I keep it with me so I can review various verses whenever I have a minute. What's the best way you've found to memorize the Prince's word? (If you haven't found the Church's scripture mastery app, that's also a great place to start!) I promise you, the more verses you can make your own, the stronger your ability will be to use that powerful sword the moment you need it.

Another thing we need to remember is that spiritual rebirth and the baptism of fire won't bring us to a state of complete and total sinlessness. (Jesus Christ is the only one who was able to live that way in mortality.) So what can we really expect in our battle with sin? You may enjoy reading what the Apostle John said about that in 1 John 3:9 and 5:18. Make sure to examine the footnotes and compare the original version of each verse with the Joseph Smith Translation.

In these scriptures, John teaches that even after we're born again and baptized by fire, we'll still occasionally give way to sin. But the difference is, once we're born again, we "cannot *continue* in sin" (1 John 3:9, footnote b; from Joseph Smith Translation; emphasis added). Imagine what a joy it will be to finally put an end our continuous battle with sin and the shame, guilt, and despair that go along with it! Really, that's what this whole fight was all about.

A PRINCE'S KINGDOM

GET READY TO crank up that wonderful imagination of yours once again, because the golden gates of our Prince's kingdom are rising up before us. What a long journey to get here! There's been so much to repent of, turn from, and overcome. And yet it was all worth it in the end because we came to know our magnificent Prince, and through His grace, we were spiritually reborn and baptized by fire. Now that we've arrived at the entrance to His kingdom, we wonder what it will take to enter in.

As we study the majestic gates, we see an archway overhead that bears the striking words *The Kingdom of Zion*. But before we jump to any conclusions, let's remember that the term *Zion* can actually represent a number of things. First, Zion can refer to the New Jerusalem, a city to be built in Jackson County, Missouri, before the Second Coming of the Lord (see D&C 57:1–2; 84:2). Since this future city hasn't been established yet, we know this can't be it. In addition, Zion can also represent the Lord's modern-day Church, or The Church of Jesus Christ of Latter-day Saints (see D&C 68:25–26; 107:36–37.) And yet, even with our membership in hand, we find the gates unwilling to budge.

However, if we continue to ponder the concept of Zion, we'll recall a passage of scripture that contains a phrase written in capital letters, as if to give the words extra special emphasis. Thankfully,

in this one short verse, we'll find exactly what we're looking for: "Therefore, verily, thus saith the Lord, let Zion rejoice, for this is Zion—THE PURE IN HEART" (D&C 97:21). Now we know who inhabits the kingdom behind these lofty walls—and we also know how to enter in.

If the land of Zion consists of the pure in heart, then that means the gates open only to those who have been "spiritually . . . born of God," "received his image in [their] countenances," and "experienced this mighty change in [their] hearts" (Alma 5:14). Remember, the Lord Himself told Nicodemus, "Except a man be born again, he cannot see the kingdom of God" (John 3:3). This was an eye-opening revelation for me, since I'd spent most of my life trying to enter Zion by my Church work and outward gospel service. No wonder I'd never made it through the imposing gates!

The Pharisees felt the same frustration as they sought to enter this particular kingdom:

> And when he was demanded of the Pharisees, when the kingdom of God should come, he answered them and said, The kingdom of God cometh not with observation:
>
> Neither shall they say, Lo here! or, lo there! for, behold, the kingdom of God has already come unto you. (Luke 17:20–21, footnote b; from Joseph Smith Translation)

Zion had been there all along, only the Pharisees had missed it. Though they'd spent their time in the temple and the synagogue fulfilling all the intricate duties of their religion, still the Jewish leaders failed to recognize that Zion in its truest sense lies in the hidden recesses of the heart. As President Spencer W. Kimball taught when he quoted the words of Brigham Young, "Zion 'commences in the heart of each person.'"[1] Once that truth settles deep into our souls, we'll find entrance into this kingdom, not through our performance but through our repentance, which allowed our hearts to be purified in a baptism of fire.

For this reason, the gates of Zion will now swing open right before our eyes. As we begin to explore this incredible paradise, I believe you'll find it unlike any place you've ever known. While other lands may boast elaborate gardens and lush landscapes, this

particular city exists for a different reason. In short, it's a sanctuary for our heart—a brand-new home for the brand-new person we've become. Unlike an outward kingdom with its concrete city walls and streets paved with gold, this extraordinary realm can only be experienced through the eyes and ears of our spirit. But even though it's invisible to the outside world, don't think for a minute that it's hard for us to see. All we have to do is make sure we're looking through the right pair of eyes.

In Zion, we'll finally be free from the misery and chains of the dragon's lair. Here we'll receive "peace . . . as a river, and . . . righteousness as the waves of the sea" (1 Nephi 20:18). Behind the protection of these walls, our enemy "shall have no power over [us] to drag [us] down to the gulf of misery and endless wo" (Helaman 5:12). Instead, we'll "stand fast . . . in the liberty wherewith Christ hath made us free" (Galatians 5:1). Best of all, as we "delight [ourselves]" in the Lord, "he shall give [us] the desires of [our] heart" (Psalm 37:4). In short, we'll experience great exhilaration as we glimpse the treasures that await us in this wonderful kingdom.

I think one of the coolest things we'll find once we enter Zion is a brand-new ability to see life solely through the eyes of our Prince. Just like a newly healed blind woman enjoying her first sunrise, we too will begin to see our entire existence in whole new light. This extraordinary vision will not only lift our sights and enlarge our perspective but also melt away all confusion and infuse our minds with insight. Suddenly we'll view each day not through our previously limited mortal perspective, but from the magnificent point of view of the Prince.

So what is it that Jesus's eyes see? Simply put, they picture the miraculous (John 14:12). They see beyond the wind and the waves (Matthew 14:28–31). They notice the lilies and the sparrows (Luke 12:27; Matthew 10:29). And they view adversity without flinching (1 Nephi 19:9). And these incredible eyes can be ours if we'll allow Christ to match our sights to those found within the limitless kingdom of Zion.

In fact, because our Prince has such awesome things in store for us, it's vital we learn to see things as He sees them, or we'll be left to wallow in hesitation, apprehension, or outright fear. After all, consider some of the outlandish and irrational things the Lord has asked of His servants in the past. For Noah, the task required building an ark three stories high and longer than a football field (Genesis 6:14–15). For Lehi, the direction involved taking his family into the desert and then crossing uncharted waters to a new land (1 Nephi 2:2). For Joshua, the invitation came to fight a battle with only a march and a shout (Joshua 6). And for Daniel, the opportunity arose to stand up for his principles amid the threat of a lions' den (Daniel 6). Could such challenging and even illogical tasks be waiting for us as well?

If so, we can learn a lot from these ancient prophets. How did Noah find the faith to construct such a colossus in his backyard? How did Lehi lead his family into the wild unknown? How did Joshua convince his army to conquer Jericho in such an odd way? And how did Daniel face the lions, void of any fear? The answer: each man was granted the empowering, enlightening, encouraging vision of the Prince. As these great men turned from their own limited, mortal perspective and viewed their assignment through His eyes, they were able to face their difficult tasks with a tremendous amount of courage and an abundant measure of faith.

Stories like these aren't just fairy tales, you know. They invite us to step into our own new world of faith, for once we settle into our Prince's kingdom, we too will perform extraordinary feats, we too will watch the Lord fight our battles in new and unusual ways, and we too will face adversity with boldness and bravery. But these possibilities can only become realities when we see them through the eyes of our Savior. Once our eyes are opened to His glorious perspective, our lives will resemble those in the scriptures as we're empowered to believe the unbelievable, embrace the irrational, and yes, even accomplish the impossible.

For instance, I'll never forget the summer I felt a strong prompting that I needed to write a book. I struggled with that impression because I'd been out of college for almost twenty years. In all that time, I'd never written anything more complicated than a journal entry. As a result, the prospect of a manuscript loomed even larger than Noah's ark. But as the Lord gently invited me to look through His eyes, I could finally see what He was envisioning.

At that moment, all my reservations fell away, and I found myself filled with desire to do exactly what He'd asked. In the end, the experience stretched and blessed me far beyond anything I could ever have imagined.

What I eventually realized is that we'll never be able to understand this Prince of ours with our logical, rational minds. During the Lord's earthly ministry, even His own disciples at times marveled over His puzzling words and unpredictable ways (see John 6:52–66). Faced with their inability to make sense of His teachings, Jesus's followers were left to plead for help to see things through His eyes. Sadly, those who couldn't do so eventually "went back, and walked no more with him" (verse 66).

Why can our Prince be so confusing at times? One reason might be because the plan that seems the most logical to us is not always the one He'll choose to pursue. In the Book of Mormon, Alma and Amulek faced this irony in the concluding moments of their mission (Alma 14). Tragically, in the people's final rejection of the missionaries' message, the unbelievers decided to gather the families of the believers and "cast [them] into the fire" (verse 8). Please note, they threw the "women and children" into the blaze (verse 10). *The women and children.* And so I ask: Wouldn't the Lord's course of action seem almost inevitable? The innocent were suffering horrible deaths! Could there be any greater time for our Prince to come to His servants' aid? Surprisingly, He chose not to do so. Alma and Amulek were instead constrained to watch the martyrdom in anguish and sorrow (verses 9–11).

Those surveying that awful scene through mortal eyes may have concluded that the Lord had forsaken His believers, or that He was powerless against the conspiring designs of the wicked. While that may have been how the situation *looked*, it's definitely not how our Prince chose to see it (verse 11). Because Alma and Amulek were able to see the situation as the Lord saw it, they understood. And it was that perspective that enabled the two men to endure without crumbling. Amid their sadness and pain, the missionaries were empowered to view the heartrending situation solely through the eyes of their wise and all-knowing Savior.

Thankfully, the citizens of Zion receive solemn promises, truths upon which they can rely when the heavens seem silent. One is the assurance that the Lord "will never leave [us], nor forsake [us]" (Hebrews 13:5). Another is the promise that He will strengthen us and help us (Isaiah 41:10). Still another is that He will not forget us, for He has "graven [us] upon the palms of [His] hands" (1 Nephi 21:15–16).

As our minds grab hold of these comforting truths, all our worry, anxiety, and fear will quickly fade away. Like the timid servant of Elisha who trembled as he observed the vast enemy host, once the Lord opens our eyes to see the "the mountain . . . full of horses and chariots of fire" (2 Kings 6:17), we too will be "delivered . . . from all [our] fears" (Psalm 34:4). Once our perspective changes, we'll discover that it no longer matters if bad things seem to be happening all around us. We won't doubt, fret, or panic. We'll simply view these things with newly enlightened vision and a heart full of ever-increasing faith.

Could you use a new pair of eyes? Would you like to see things as the Prince sees them? If so, then you've come to the right place, for only in Zion can the "scales of darkness . . . begin to fall from [our] eyes" (2 Nephi 30:6). Only here can our "eyes [be] opened, and [our] understanding quickened" (D&C 138:29). Only here can we truly "see the kingdom of God coming in power and great glory unto [our] deliverance" (D&C 56:18). And that's only the beginning of what we'll find in the incomparable kingdom of our incomparable Prince.

For Additional Study

Read Doctrine and Covenants 58:3; Moses 1:11; and Moses 6:35–36. Have you ever considered that it's not just difficult to understand God with our "natural eyes," but it's actually impossible?

In his Gospel, the Apostle John often recorded what happened when people tried to understand Christ through their own logical reasoning. If you want to read some of these accounts, you can turn to John 2:18–21; 3:3–4; 4:10–12, 31–33; 6:40–66; 8:31–36, 51–53; 9:39–41; and 11:11–15.

When it comes to the Lord's involvement in our own lives, isn't it possible that we will encounter the same problem? Can you see the need for us to view our Savior's words through *His* eyes and not through our own natural ones?

When the time for His atoning sacrifice finally came, how rational was it for the disciples to watch their powerful Leader hang on the cross? How do you think His agonizing death appeared to their limited mortal view? To capture the true irony of the situation, read Matthew 27:39–43 and Luke 23:35–37. What was it that enlarged the Apostles' vision so they could see this seeming tragedy with an eternal perspective?

Finally, here are a few glimpses of what can happen when the citizens of Zion are invited to look through the all-encompassing eyes of their Prince: 1 Nephi 11–14; D&C 138; and Moses 1:1–11.

AN ENDOWMENT OF POWER

BE HONEST: HAS all this talk about living extraordinary lives and doing extraordinary things left you feeling a little skeptical? I wouldn't be surprised. We know that "with God all things are possible" (Matthew 19:26), but sometimes our reality just doesn't match that glowing description. Instead, all that stuff about building arks, crossing deserts, and facing lions seems to belong more to the scriptural world than our normal, everyday lives. So we simply read the stories, never dreaming we could actually live out such adventures for ourselves.

Besides, even if we wanted to believe the unbelievable and accomplish the impossible, we may worry that our limited capacity could never live up to the Lord's sweeping views and intimidating tasks. Because we've lived so long with our various weaknesses and inadequacies, perhaps it's easier to conclude we're simply not the scriptural superhero type.

Well, all that is about to change now that we've entered the land of Zion.

We've definitely experienced some amazing things so far in our princess story, but we've saved the best for last. In this delightful and enchanting city, we're going to encounter a whole new way of living—one I think is nothing short of magical. Simply put, you now find yourself in a world where miracles aren't a rare occurrence but a natural part of everyday life.

To show you what I mean, let's turn first to a promise of the Lord found in over twenty-five different places in the Book of Mormon. I'm guessing you've read it several times before: "Inasmuch as ye shall keep my commandments ye shall prosper in the land; and inasmuch as ye will not keep my commandments ye shall be cut off from my presence" (2 Nephi 4:4; see also Mosiah 2:22; Alma 9:14; and Alma 37:13).

Just in case this verse has become a little too familiar to you, I want you to look again at what our Savior is actually promising. He says that those who obey Him will *prosper*, which means "to be successful or fortunate" or to "thrive" or "flourish."[1] Notice that He doesn't say we'll "sometimes" thrive or we'll "occasionally" flourish. No, our Prince proclaims *continual* prosperity as a gift for all who are willing to keep His commandments. Sounds like a pretty wonderful life for those who enter the blessed kingdom of Zion.

In this same verse, the Lord also reveals exactly how such abundant prosperity will be possible. When He says that those who refuse to keep His commandments will be "cut off from [His] presence," He's also telling us the faithful will have His presence to be with them continually. And if our Hero is with us every moment of every day, we can rest assured that our lives are going to prosper. His companionship is all we'll need to thrive and flourish in a big way.

As remarkable as this blessing is, you may wonder like I did how we can prosper when mortality will continue to plague us with all different kinds of adversity. How do we flourish or thrive with all the challenges and afflictions life brings? We may think the only way we can do so is to have our Prince remove all our difficulty and hardship once and for all. But the truth is that our Prince had something much bigger in mind when He brought us to Zion. You're about to learn a wonderful secret about life in this land, and just like I said, it involves a daily dose of *magic* and *miracles*.

One of my favorite Christian authors, Hannah Whitall Smith, captures it beautifully in her book *The Christian's Secret to a Happy Life*. (I hope you don't mind her old-fashioned 1800s language.

I find it fascinating!) Pay close attention as she describes a new way of dealing with adversity for those who live in the Prince's kingdom:

> The only idea the human heart can compass, is, that outward circumstances must bend and bow to the soul that is seated on a throne with Christ. Friends must approve, enemies must be silenced, obstacles must be overcome, [and] affairs must prosper. . . . If man had had the ordering of Daniel's business, or of that matter of [Shadrach, Meshach, and Abednego] in the burning fiery furnace, he would have said the only way of victory would be for the minds of the kings to have been so changed that Daniel should not have been cast into the den of lions, and the Hebrew children should have been kept out of the furnace. But God's way was infinitely grander. He suffered Daniel to be cast among the lions, in order that he might reign triumphant over them when in their very midst, and He allowed Shadrach, Meshach, and Abednego to be cast into the burning, fiery furnace, *in order that they might walk through it without so much as the smell of fire upon them.* He tells us, not that we shall walk in path where there are no dragons and [snakes], *but that we shall walk through the midst of dragons and [snakes], and shall "tread them under our feet."*[2]

That's pretty amazing stuff if you ask me. All our lives, we've believed that the only way we could be happy is by having all our problems and challenges taken away for good. But like Ms. Smith said, our Prince's plan is "infinitely grander" than that. Wouldn't you say it's a much greater miracle, rather than escaping our trials, to be given the strength to rise up and triumph right in the middle of them? That's the last thing any normal person would be able to do, which makes it all the more miraculous. Can you even imagine having access to that kind of power in your daily life? I can't think of any better way for us to prosper. We're talking about lions being tamed and fiery furnaces not even burning someone's skin. I know it sounds like something out of a Harry Potter movie, but it's not. It's the magic we'll experience every single day of our lives as privileged citizens of the Prince's magnificent kingdom.

A great example of this kind of prosperity is found in the pages of the Old Testament. When Joseph was sold into Egypt by his brothers, he faced a great deal of hardship, so you'd think his life was anything but magical or miraculous. But if you look a little closer at the details of his story, you'll see the incredible truth. Genesis 39 says, "The Lord was with Joseph, and he was a *prosperous* man . . . and his master saw that *the Lord was with him*, and that the Lord *made all that he did to prosper* in his hand" (Genesis 39:2–3; emphasis added). Though he lived as a slave, the scriptures describe Joseph as prosperous because the Prince was "with him" no matter what he was doing.

Even when Potiphar's wife tried to seduce him and Joseph was unfairly sent to prison, the young man still continued to prosper, for again, "*the Lord was with Joseph*, and shewed him mercy, and *gave him favour* in the sight of the keeper of the prison" (Genesis 39:21; emphasis added). Eventually even the keeper of the prison noticed that "the Lord was with [Joseph], and that which he did, the Lord made it to *prosper*" (Genesis 39:23; emphasis added). Tell me, would you like to live your life the same way Joseph did? Would you like to prosper right in the middle of even the toughest adversity? If so, there's only one way you can do it. If you'll keep your Prince with you continually, your life really will flourish like the ancient prophet Joseph's did.

I think one reason we may have been deprived of this privilege in the past is because we've assumed that our precious Savior could only be with us during our "spiritual" times, like when we're reading our scriptures, saying our prayers, or sitting in church. But that's not how life works in the Prince's kingdom at all. For goodness' sake, He joined Joseph right in the depths of a dungeon! So that means He can be with us in the middle of our most gloomy, chaotic, and messy moments. Not only will He will be with us, but because He is, everything will work out okay. Actually, it will be better than okay. Just like Joseph, as long as we stay close to our precious Prince, every single thing we do will *prosper*. And it won't be because we're strong, faithful, and amazing—it will be because *He* is. In fact, our Hero is so powerful that His light will shine even brighter the worse our adversity gets.

I love how the prophet Jeremiah wraps this truth into a descriptive little analogy. He tells us that those who refuse to trust in the Lord will be like a tree in the desert—a tree that "shall inhabit the parched places in the wilderness, in a salt land and not inhabited" (Jeremiah 17:6). In other words, those who live without Christ will struggle in the wasteland of depression, hopelessness, fear, insecurity, and despair. But Jeremiah says those who trust in their Prince will be "as a tree planted by the waters, and that spreadeth out her roots by the river," and this tree "shall not [fear] when heat cometh, but her leaf shall be green; and . . . in the year of drought, . . . shall [not] cease from yielding fruit" (verse 8; see footnote b). Did you catch the amazing prosperity in the last part of that verse? Even when heat tries to blister her leaves and drought tries to dry out her roots (meaning she experiences really difficult adversity), this vibrant tree doesn't wilt in the least. She prospers through it all for one reason and one reason only—because she's continually drinking in the living water of her Lord.

I hope you're beginning to catch the vision of life in this extraordinary kingdom. Only our Prince can grant us this kind of powerful inner victory right in the middle of our trials and afflictions. It's a life of magic and miracles far beyond anything we've ever experienced. As astonishing as it may be, I want you to take a deep breath, because there's something even greater waiting for us on the path up ahead. Believe it or not, we're on the verge of discovering the ultimate privilege available to the citizens of Zion.

In your mind's eye, can you picture something shining like a beacon from the top of the next hill? It's our Prince's magnificent palace. Constructed of the finest materials available, this glorious building exudes majesty and elegance from the bottom of its foundation to the top of its glistening spires. However, it's not the outward beauty of the edifice that draws our attention at this moment. Our focus rests on what's waiting behind the exquisite façade.

What in the world is so special about our Prince's house? The answer is one of the most mind-blowing parts of living in the kingdom of Zion. All who enter the temple are invited to receive their *own* endowment. An endowment simply means a gift. Our Savior offers this glorious inheritance to all those who reside in His personal kingdom. However, this rich endowment doesn't consist of gold or land like other kings bestow. No, it's a grant of even greater wealth, for "in [the Prince's] house," He "endow[s] those whom [He has] chosen with *power from on high*" (D&C 95:8; emphasis added). Truly, only in our Prince's magnificent temple can we obtain the highest blessings available in all the land.

I'm guessing you'd like to hear more about this one-of-a-kind endowment. Well, first I can tell you it's an even greater gift of our Savior's enabling grace. While we've already experienced what it's like to be filled with our Prince's grace, the endowment of power available in His temple will carry us to higher heights and greater possibilities than anything we've seen thus far. The Lord Himself described it as a "blessing such as is not known among the children of men" (D&C 39:15; see also D&C 38:31–32). To sum it up, when we obtain this endowment, a new power will live within us that will affect not only our lives but also the lives of every single person we come in contact with.

For instance, take Ammon's incredible story in the Book of Mormon. It's a perfect example of what can happen once we've been endowed with the power of our Prince. Faced with the challenge of the king's scattered flocks, Ammon knew he could rely on the special power living deep inside him. Notice how he said, "I will show forth my power . . . *or the power which is in me* . . . that I may win the hearts of these my fellow-servants . . . to believe in my words" (Alma 17:29). He then demonstrated that power by taking out an entire band of Lamanite thugs all by himself, leaving nothing but a bunch of chopped-off arms in his wake. In fact, the power Ammon displayed was so far beyond a man's normal ability, King Lamoni thought he was the Great Spirit come to earth in human form (see Alma 18:1–4). But don't forget that Ammon's spectacular feat wasn't just for show. Instead, it served to open the door for the conversion of an entire Lamanite community (Alma 19). Could there be a better example of what can happen once we're endowed with the almighty power of our Prince?

Of course, Ammon wasn't the only one who displayed the astonishing power we'll receive through our Savior's endowment. The scriptures actually point out several of Zion's citizens who exhibited the same kind of jaw-dropping results. Daniel, Peter,

Paul, and Nephi all possessed such extraordinary strength and ability, others were tempted to fall down and worship at their feet (see Daniel 2:46; Acts 10:25–26; 14:11; 28:3–6; and 1 Nephi 17:55). Yet as powerful as these men were, they really weren't that different from you and me. They struggled with the same weaknesses, infirmities, and frailties that plague our lives (see Acts 14:14–15; 2 Corinthians 12:7–10; 2 Nephi 4:17–19; and Alma 26:12). The difference is that they trusted so completely in their endowment of princely power, their contribution to the Lord's work was nothing short of miraculous!

As this scene comes to a close, then, I have to ask: As newly healed and grace-filled daughters of God, could it be our turn to make our own miraculous contributions? Could it be our turn to experience what our scriptural heroes experienced? Could it be our turn to rise to new heights of greatness rather than watching the animated princesses do so on the movie screen? The scriptures assure us that such a thing is possible—but only if we prepare ourselves to enter the Prince's house and embrace the endowment of power found therein.

Once we do, we too will find the strength to leave our own legacy and work our own miracles. We too will do things we're not capable of doing, know things we wouldn't otherwise know, and manifest more strength than we ever thought possible. And it's all made possible through the extraordinary power of our Prince.

For Additional Study

Let's go to the Old Testament (since we're not quite as familiar with these stories) and see if we can find this wonderful magic in the lives of people who lived so long ago. As you read through the following passages, put yourself in their shoes and try to imagine what it felt like to experience the miracles they experienced through the power of their Prince: Exodus 14; Judges 6–7; 2 Kings 6:24–25; and 7:1–16 (especially verse 6).

Now let's look at two stories found back-to-back in the Book of Mormon. Both groups of people were in bondage (meaning they were experiencing difficult adversity), but the Lord chose to deliver the groups in different ways. Read Mosiah 21–24. (I know

that's a lot, but this is an amazing part of the Book of Mormon!) After studying these chapters, tell me, who experienced the true magic in their deliverance? Which group prospered right in the midst of their adversity? And most important, how can these two stories apply to your individual challenges and trials?

In the Book of Mormon, Nephi paints a beautiful picture of the power-filled life we've been talking about. To catch just a glimpse, look up the following scriptures and see how the young prophet prospered through many different trials and challenges: 1 Nephi 4; 16:18–32; 17. As these scriptures clearly show, with our Prince's power gracing our every thought and action, truly nothing will be impossible.

For a final example, read through the familiar story of the stripling warriors in Alma 56. Then answer the following questions (and record your answers in your journal): How did the Lord prosper these young men through their adversity? Why didn't the other Nephites receive a similar miracle? What do you think made the difference between the stripling warriors and the other Nephite soldiers? How can this story relate to your personal life?

A HAPPILY EVER AFTER

WELL, BELOVED PRINCESS, it's finally time to wrap up our story. It's been quite an incredible saga, wouldn't you say? Full of magic and adventure, dangerous monsters and an evil villain, and an incredibly daring rescue at the hands of a handsome Prince. But at the heart of this story is the same thing that's at the heart of every princess story. When all is said and done, this tale has really been an incredibly beautiful *love story*. At least, I hope that's what it's become for you. I hope that just like the movie princesses, you've found a love greater than any you've experienced in your entire life.

That love you feel for your Prince—and His love for you—is what will bring us to our happily ever after, for truly your greatest joy and fulfillment will only come as you're "clasped in the arms of Jesus" (Mormon 5:11). Like Nephi, I pray you too have been "filled . . . with his love, even unto the consuming of [your] flesh" (2 Nephi 4:21) and that you really are "rooted and grounded" in His transforming and life-changing love (Ephesians 3:17).

It's what your Prince has been hoping for all along. Through every single scene of our story, He's been there to care for you, cleanse you, and save you from the villain's lies. Again and again He's invited you to spend time with Him so you could draw closer to Him and get to know Him. And by this point, if you're not experiencing your own magnificent love story, then the journey we've taken has all been for naught. That's because the love of Christ truly is "most sweet, above all that [we] ever before tasted" (1 Nephi 8:11). It really is "most desirable above all things" and "the most joyous to the soul" (1 Nephi 11:22–23).

Perhaps you never really thought of your Prince as the greatest love of your life. Perhaps in earlier years, you admired Him from afar or appreciated what He did for you, but you often went days without thinking about Him and weeks without taking the time to draw close Him. But after everything you've been through, I desperately hope all that has changed. I hope you're so enamored with your Hero that you can hardly go a minute without His wondrous presence right by your side.

It's funny—we're all familiar with the concept of falling head over heels in love with someone, but we often forget that we can apply that idea to our relationship with our Prince. I'm completely serious. Think for a minute about what it feels like when you fall in love. Thoughts of that person begin to overtake your mind, and you're filled with irresistible feelings of admiration and affection. You long to be with that person, to know more about them, and to do all you can to please and delight them. In short, their every wish is your command. I believe that perfectly captures what can happen in our relationship with our Prince. At least, President Ezra Taft Benson described it that way when he spoke of those who were spiritually born of God:

> Men captained by Christ will be consumed in Christ. . . . Their will is swallowed up in his will. They do always those things that please the Lord. Not only would they die for the Lord, but, more important, they want to live for Him. . . . They have Christ on their minds, as they look unto Him in every thought. They have Christ in their hearts as their affections are placed on Him forever. . . . In short, they lose themselves in the Lord and find eternal life.[1]

Tell me, sweet princess, is Christ on your mind continually while you go about your day? Are the affections of your heart placed on Him forever? Do you look to Him in every thought and lose yourself in His incomparable love? Simply put, are you

"captained by Christ" and "consumed in Christ" just like President Benson said?

Ever since the world began, the Lord's most important commandment—the one that stands above all His other commands—has been that we "love [Him] with all [our] heart, and with all [our] soul, and with all [our] mind" (Matthew 22:36–37; see also Deuteronomy 6:5; Mark 12:30; Luke 10:27; and D&C 59:5). Notice that He could have said we must "follow" Him, or "serve" Him, or "obey" Him with all our heart, soul, and mind—but He didn't. That's because He wasn't interested in gaining a follower, a servant, or a worker bee. *He wanted a love story.* In fact, He died for you to show how much He loves you. Oh, how I hope He's taken His place as the true love of your life and that you've given Him your whole heart in return. There really is nothing like losing yourself in a beautiful relationship of love that will last for the rest of eternity. Your Hero deserves nothing less than all your heart and soul.

Believe it or not, your Prince has actually invited you to participate in a ceremony where you'll be able to pledge your love to Him by covenant. And where else would such a blessed ceremony take place than within the walls of His holy house? It's another wonderful part of receiving our endowment in the palace of the Prince. The temple endowment is actually similar to a marriage ceremony because it's there we promise to give our lives wholly and completely to our wondrous Prince.

In other words, when we make sacred covenants in the temple, we're really "yielding [our] hearts" to our beloved Savior (Helaman 3:35). To *yield* means "to give up or surrender (oneself)."[2] One way we could look at it is through the word *consecration*. As Elder Neal A. Maxwell taught, "We tend to think of consecration only as yielding up, when divinely directed, our material possessions. *But ultimate consecration is the yielding up of oneself to God.*"[3]

I love how one author compares this kind of consecration to biblical times when a king chose a woman to be his wife. Here's how he describes it:

Consecrate means "to sanctify," and *sanctify* means "to set apart." A good example of this would be a woman selected to become the wife of a king. She would be brought into the palace where the king's eunuchs would care for her. The eunuchs' responsibility would be to prepare her for the king. No longer would she live a normal life, as other women would, for she was consecrated, sanctified, or set apart for the king. However, if she cooperated, the sanctification would be a small price compared to the tremendous benefits she would receive. She would enjoy intimate privileges with the king no one else would share. All that he had would be hers. In return, what did the king expect from her? She was to be his, only his.[4]

I hope you can see that all along the Lord has wanted nothing less than for you to be set apart for Him and Him alone. He's wanted you to hold nothing back in your relationship with Him, just like He's held nothing back from you. When you covenant to consecrate yourself to your Prince in the temple, it's your way of showing Him that your heart is fully and completely His—now and forevermore.

Truly, there's no better way for us to live happily ever after. After all, what could be better than to "feast upon his love" (Jacob 3:2) even "until [we] are filled" (Alma 32:42)? Royal princess, I promise you that once you taste of your Prince's deeply satisfying love, your life will never be the same again. You'll join the Psalmist in saying, "My heart is fixed" (Psalm 57:7), "My soul followeth hard after thee" (Psalm 63:8), and "My tongue also shall talk of thy righteousness all the day long" (Psalm 71:24). Truly, Christ has "loved [us] with an everlasting love" (Jeremiah 31:3), a love that surpasses every other type of love we could ever experience.

If it's going to be a while before you can go through the temple, I have some great news for you. You don't have to wait until you receive your endowment to offer your heart to your Prince. Instead, you can do exactly what they used to do in the days of Christ when two people wanted to give their life to each other by covenant. In the Jewish world, a couple actually began their relationship by being *betrothed*.

Now, a betrothal wasn't the same as being engaged, where the couple can still break up at any time and it's acceptable. It was much more serious than that. In Jewish culture, if a man was interested in a young woman as his bride, he first paid her father a "bride price," or a *mohar* as the Jews called it.[5] (I hope you're thinking about the price Christ has already paid to redeem you or buy you back from the enemy!) That sealed the deal, and the couple was then technically seen as husband and wife, only they weren't allowed to live together just yet. This stage often lasted up to a year and gave the couple time to make preparations for the full and complete covenant of marriage.

So if you're not quite old enough to go through the temple, you could simply consider yourself betrothed to your Prince, meaning you're preparing in every way to give your heart to Him when you go to the temple. Remember, in the waters of baptism you already promised that you were "willing to take upon [you] the name of [the] Son, and always remember him" (D&C 20:77). Sounds a lot like preparing for a marriage covenant if you ask me. You're preparing in every way to give yourself wholly to Him, like a woman who was set apart to be the wife of a king. Now that you know your Prince intimately and you've experienced His breathtaking love, it really will be the gift you most want to give Him—the gift of your newly healed and newly restored princess heart.

In fact, King Benjamin speaks clearly of the time when "Christ, the Lord God Omnipotent, may *seal you his*" (Mosiah 5:15; emphasis added). I think that's the best news you could ever receive when it comes to your Prince, for you really are "complete in him" (Colossians 2:10). He is all you'll ever need and more. I hope by now you're starting to feel the same way.

As the storyteller, I'd like to use our final moments together to share with you how I personally feel about my extraordinary Prince. Like Nephi, I too can say that I "glory in my Jesus" (2 Nephi 33:6), for He has become "my strength and my song; he also has become my salvation" (2 Nephi 22:2). He's my strength because He's given me the power to rise up over temptation and the self-control I could never muster up on my own. He's my song because He's my joy, my happiness, and my sunshine, no matter what else is going on around me. And He's my salvation because He continues to keep me safe from the wiles of the villain and transform me into the woman I was always meant to become. I love Him in a way that's extremely difficult to put into words.

More than anything, I hope our story has helped you realize that this same glorious love is available to every royal princess who chooses to turn from the things of the world and come unto Christ. If by chance your heart isn't yet swelling with love for your magnificent Prince, don't worry. This princess story is one that can be told and retold from now until the end of time. So if you need to, go right back to the beginning and take the opportunity to find your blessed Prince all over again. I promise, it's the only way you'll truly live happily ever after.

 "And ye shall seek me, and find me, when ye shall search for me with all your heart." (Jeremiah 29:13)

ENDNOTES

A Royal Obsession

1. "Wedding of Prince William and Catherine Middleton," *Wikipedia*, accessed October 28, 2014, http://en.wikipedia.org/wiki/Wedding_of_Prince_William_and_Catherine_Middleton#Public_celebration.

2. "Tangled," *Wikipedia*, accessed October 28, 2014, http://en.wikipedia.org/wiki/Tangled#Reception.

A Peculiar Princess

1. Dieter F. Uchtdorf, "Your Happily Ever After," *Ensign*, May 2010; emphasis added.

2. Elaine S. Dalton, "Remember Who You Are!" *Ensign*, May 2010; emphasis added.

3. Dieter F. Uchtdorf, "The Love of God," *Ensign*, November 2009.

4. "Young Women Theme," LDS.org, https://www.lds.org/young-women/personal-progress/young-women-theme?lang=eng.

5. "Message from the First Presidency," *For the Strength of Youth*, LDS.org, https://www.lds.org/youth/for-the-strength-of-youth?lang=eng.

6. "Welcome to Personal Progress," *Personal Progress*, LDS.org, https://www.lds.org/young-women/personal-progress/welcome-to-personal-progress?lang=eng.

7. Ezra Taft Benson, "To the Young Women of the Church," *Ensign*, November 1986.

8. "Become," Dictionary.com, http://dictionary.reference.com/browse/become?s=t.

A Notorious Villain

1. C. S. Lewis, *Mere Christianity* (New York: Touchstone, 1996), 45–46.

2. Jeffrey R. Holland, "We Are All Enlisted," *Ensign*, November 2011.

3. John Eldredge, *Epic: The Story God Is Telling* (Nashville, TN: Thomas Nelson, 2004) 39; emphasis added.

4. Melvin J. Ballard, "Struggle for the Soul," *New Era*, March 1984.

An Awful Monster

1. "Princess and dragon," *Wikipedia*, accessed November 4, 2015, http://en.wikipedia.org/wiki/Princess_and_dragon.

2. Bible Dictionary, "Fall of Adam and Eve."

3. *Teachings of Presidents of the Church: Joseph F. Smith* (Salt Lake City: The Church of Jesus Christ of Latter-day Saints, 2011), 96.

4. Dallin H. Oaks, "The Light and the Life," *New Era*, December 1996; emphasis added.

5. Jeffrey R. Holland, "Where Justice, Love, and Mercy Meet," *Ensign*, May 2015.

A Dragon Nature

1. C. S. Lewis, *The Voyage of the Dawn Treader* (New York: HarperTrophy, 1994), 91; emphasis added.

2. Ibid., 102.

3. "Nature," Dictionary.com, http://dictionary.reference.com/browse/nature?s=t.

4. "Nature," Thesaurus.com, http://www.thesaurus.com/browse/nature.

5. "Divine," Dictionary.com, http://dictionary.reference.com/browse/divine?s=t.

6. *Teachings of the Presidents of the Church: Joseph F. Smith* (Salt Lake City: The Church of Jesus Christ of Latter-day Saints, 2011), 96.

7. "Subject," Dictionary.com, http://dictionary.reference.com/browse/subject?s=t.

8. C. S. Lewis, *The Voyage of the Dawn Treader* (New York: HarperTrophy, 1994), 114–15.

An Awe-Inspiring Hero

1. "Redeem," Dictionary.com, http://dictionary.reference.com/browse/redeem?s=t.

2. Bible Dictionary, "Gospel."

3. Dallin H. Oaks, "Faith in the Lord Jesus Christ," *Ensign*, May 1994.

4. Ezra Taft Benson, "Jesus Christ: Our Savior and Redeemer," *Ensign*, June 1990; emphasis added.

5. Thomas S. Monson, "The Search For Jesus," *Ensign*, December 1990.

6. Ezra Taft Benson, "Come unto Christ," *Ensign*, November 1987.

7. Ibid.

8. F. Enzio Busche, "The Only Real Treasure," *New Era*, December 1979.

9. Henry B. Eyring, "That We May Be One," *Ensign*, May 1998.

10. Brigham Young, in *Journal of Discourses* (London: F. D. Richards, 1855), 8:339.

A Dangerous Distraction

1. Russell M. Nelson, "Repentance and Conversion," *Ensign*, May 2007; emphasis in original.

2. Dieter F. Uchtdorf, "Is There a Point of No Return?" *New Era*, June 2010.

3. "Change," Thesaurus.com, http://www.thesaurus.com/browse/change?s=t.

4. Timothy Keller, *Counterfeit Gods: The Empty Promises of Money, Sex, and Power, and the Only Hope that Matters* (New York: Dutton, 2009), xvii–iii.

5. Ezra Taft Benson, "A Mighty Change of Heart," *Ensign*, October 1989.

A Load of Lies

1. Modern-day scriptures teach that the little children in our families are covered by the Lord's Atonement and are not responsible for their actions until they reach the age of accountability (for example, see Moroni 8 and D&C 137:10).

2. Mindy Raye Friedman, "Truth, Lies, and Your Self-Worth," *New Era*, January 2014; emphasis in original.

3. Jeffrey R. Holland, "Come unto Me," *Ensign*, April 1998.

4. Boyd K. Packer, "A Message to the Youth of the Church: Personal Revelation—The Gift, the Test, and the Promise," *New Era*, January 1995; emphasis added.

5. James E. Faust, "The Forces That Will Save Us," *Ensign*, January 2007.

A Broken Heart

1. Bible Dictionary, "Grace."

2. Sheri Dew, *Amazed by Grace* (Salt Lake City: Deseret Book, 2015), 24–25.

3. James Strong, *Strongest Strong's Exhaustive Concordance of the Bible* (Grand Rapids, MI: Zondervan, 2001), 1571.

4. Bruce D. Porter, "A Broken Heart and a Contrite Spirit," *Ensign*, November 2007.

5. Gerald N. Lund, "Salvation: By Grace or by Works?" *Ensign*, April 1981.

6. Ezra Taft Benson, "A Mighty Change of Heart," *Ensign*, October 1989.

7. Brad Wilcox, "His Grace Is Sufficient," *Ensign*, September 2013.

A Closer Look

1. "Aslan," *Wikipedia*, http://en.wikipedia.org/wiki/Aslan.

2. C. S. Lewis, *The Voyage of the Dawn Treader* (New York: HarperTrophy, 1952), 115–16.

3. Richard G. Scott, "Finding Happiness," *BYU Speeches*, August 19, 1997, https://speeches.byu.edu/talks/richard-g-scott_
finding-happiness/.

4. Ezra Taft Benson, "Beware of Pride," *Ensign*, May 1989.

5. Ibid.

6. Dieter F. Uchtdorf, "What Is Truth?" Young Adult fireside, January 13, 2013, https://www.lds.org/broadcasts/article/print/ces-devotionals/2013/01/what-is-truth?lang=eng.

7. Gordon B. Hinckley, "Thou Shalt Not Covet," *Ensign*, March 1990.

8. "Idle," Thesaurus.com, http://www.thesaurus.com/browse/idle.

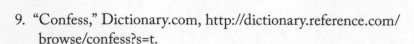

9. "Confess," Dictionary.com, http://dictionary.reference.com/browse/confess?s=t.

10. Russell M. Nelson, "Repentance and Conversion," *Ensign*, May 2007; emphasis in original.

A Great Exchange

1. W. E. Vine, *Vine's Complete Expository Dictionary of Old and New Testament Words* (Nashville, TN: Nelson, 1984), 166.

2. D. Todd Christofferson, "Justification and Sanctification," *Ensign*, June 2001.

3. Ibid.

A Baptism of Fire

1. D. Todd Christofferson, "Justification and Sanctification," *Ensign*, June 2001.

2. Ibid; emphasis in original.

3. "Fawkes," *Harry Potter Wiki*, accessed April 20, 2015, http://harrypotter.wikia.com/wiki/Fawkes.

4. D. Todd Christofferson, "Justification and Sanctification," *Ensign*, June 2001.

5. B. H. Roberts, ed., *History of the Church of Jesus Christ of Latter-day Saints*, vol. 5 (Salt Lake City: Deseret News, 1909), 499; emphasis added.

6. Boyd K. Packer, "The Gift of the Holy Ghost: What Every Member Should Know," *Ensign*, August 2006.

7. David A. Bednar, "Clean Hands and a Pure Heart," *Ensign*, November 2007.

8. David A. Bednar, "Ye Must Be Born Again," *Ensign*, May 2007.

9. Ibid.

10. "Immerse," Thesaurus.com, http://www.thesaurus.com/browse/immerse?s=t.

11. "Immerse," Dictionary.com, http://dictionary.reference.com/browse/immerse.

A Princess Warrior

1. "True," Dictionary.com, accessed November 10, 2015, http://dictionary.reference.com/browse/true?s=ts; see also "Treow," *Wicktionary*, accessed November 10, 2015, http://en.wiktionary.org/wiki/treow and Fina Cooke, "The True Story of 'True,'" Ted Ed, accessed November 10, 2015, http://ed.ted.com/lessons/the-true-story-of-true-gina-cooke.

2. "True," Thesaurus.com, http://www.thesaurus.com/browse/true.

3. "Caligae," *Wikipedia*, accessed November 11, 2015, http://en.wikipedia.org/wiki/Caligae.

4. W. E. Vine, *Vine's Complete Expository Dictionary of Old and New Testament Words* (Nashville, TN: Nelson, 1984), 483.

5. Salvation," *Merriam-Webster*, accessed November 11, 2015, http://www.merriam-webster.com/dictionary/salvation.

6. The word *quick* is also used to described the word of God in several other verses of scripture, including Helaman 3:29; D&C 6:2; 11:2; 12:2; 14:2; 27:1; and 33:1.

7. James E. Strong, *Strongest Strong's Exhaustive Concordance of the Bible* (Grand

   Rapids, MI: Zondervan, 2001), 1614.

8. W. E. Vine, *Vine's Complete Expository Dictionary of Old and New Testament Words* (Nashville, TN: Nelson, 1984), 571.

9. Ibid., 479.

10. Dieter F. Uchtdorf, "The Infinite Power of Hope," *Ensign*, November 2008.

An Epic Battle

1. Bible Dictionary, "Devil."

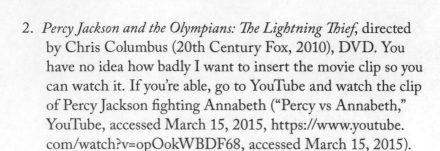

2. *Percy Jackson and the Olympians: The Lightning Thief*, directed by Chris Columbus (20th Century Fox, 2010), DVD. You have no idea how badly I want to insert the movie clip so you can watch it. If you're able, go to YouTube and watch the clip of Percy Jackson fighting Annabeth ("Percy vs Annabeth," YouTube, accessed March 15, 2015, https://www.youtube.com/watch?v=opOokWBDF68, accessed March 15, 2015).

3. "Fair," Dictionary.com, http://dictionary.reference.com/browse/fair?s=t.

4. "Clear," Dictionary.com, http://dictionary.reference.com/browse/clear?s=t.

5. "Terrible," Dictionary.com, http://dictionary.reference.com/browse/terrible?s=t.

6. See Galatians 5:23, footnote b.

7. Sheri Dew, *Amazed by Grace* (Salt Lake City: Deseret Book, 2015), 16.

8. If you'd like to know more about how my Prince helped me cast off my negative body image, you can check out my book *Body Image Breakthrough: Learning to See Your Body and Your Beauty in a Whole New Light*.

9. Richard G. Scott, "The Power of Scripture," *Ensign*, November 2011.

A Prince's Kingdom

1. Spencer W. Kimball, "Becoming the Pure in Heart," *Ensign*, March 1985.

An Endowment of Power

1. "Prosper," Dictionary.com, http://dictionary.reference.com/browse/prosper?s=t.

2. Hannah Whitall Smith, *The Christian's Secret of a Happy Life* (Peabody, MA: Hendrickson, 2004), 179.

A Happily Ever After

1. Ezra Taft Benson, "Born of God," *Ensign*, July 1989.

2. "Yield," Dictionary.com, http://dictionary.reference.com/browse/yield?s=t.

3. Neal A. Maxwell, "Consecrate Thy Performance," *Ensign*, May 2002; emphasis added.

4. John Bevere, *A Heart Ablaze* (Nashville, TN: Thomas Nelson, 1999), 27.

5. "Erusin," *Wikipedia*, accessed November 12, 2015, http://en.wikipedia.org/wiki/Erusin.

ACKNOWLEDGMENTS

To the young women and leaders from the Rexburg 19th ward: I feel like you're a part of every page, every sentence, and every scene of this story. It was fun living the drama together, wasn't it? Please know that no matter where you are, your faces and smiles will be imprinted on my mind for the rest of eternity.

To Crystal, Katy, Sarah, Katherine, Wendi, and Julie: You gave up your precious time to read a rough draft and give your feedback. And with twenty-nine kids between you, that was no small feat! How do I even begin to say thank you for that? You truly are kindred spirits whose friendship I will cherish forever.

To my amazing Cedar Fort team: What a blessing you've been in my life! Emily, you first embraced the vision of this story and helped it come to life. Shawnda, it's like you peeked inside my head and saw exactly what I'd imagined for the cover. I love it! McKell and Jessica, I could never dream of having better editors. Your input and insights have been absolutely invaluable. And Kelly, I continue to rely heavily on your advice and support. Thank you all from the very bottom of my heart!

To Greg, Breck and Katelyn, Kyler, Chase, Shay and Isaac, Kimball, Kalli, and Lexi: You are my happy place. There's nowhere on earth I'd rather be than sitting around the Sunday dinner table with you. Thank you for many precious years of laughter and love.

And most of all, to my Prince: I must say that, to me, this isn't just a story—it's our story. No one has made me feel more like a princess. My heart longs to cry out with Nephi, "O Lord, I will praise thee forever; yea, my soul will rejoice in thee" (2 Nephi 4:30). Thank you for coming to my rescue.